MEMOIRS
OF A
STEELWORKER

DAVID KUCHTA

**Canal History and
Technology Press**

Published by Canal History and Technology Press

National Canal Museum
Hugh Moore Historical Park and Museums, Inc.
30 Centre Square, Easton, Pennsylvania, 18042-7743

Many of the photographs used in this volume were taken by Joseph Elliott between 1987 and 1995, some for the Historic American Engineering Record, others for the industrial history archives of the National Canal Museum, funded by Local History Grants from the Pennsylvania Historical and Museum Commission. Except where otherwise noted, all photographs used are from the industrial history collections of the National Canal Museum, Easton, Pensylvania.

Book design by Ann Bartholomew
Cover design by Stan McKenney

ISBN 0930973-17-8
Library of Congress Catalogue Card Number: 96-71775

**Canal History and
Technology Press**

National Canal Museum
Hugh Moore Historical Park and Museums, Inc.
30 Centre Square, Easton, PA 18042-7743

I dedicate this book to all the steelworkers past and present, and especially to the workers who lost their lives making the company into the Number Two Giant of the steel industry.

I also affectionately dedicate this book to my wife Theresa for all her patience and understanding down through the years.

Last but not least, I dedicate this book to my mother, Anna Zlock Kuchta, who tried and hopefully succeeded in instilling into me the importance of being fair and honest, of having an open mind and of doing my best regardless of what adversities life handed me.

CONTENTS

CONTENTS

DISCLAIMER

What I write is true to the best of my recollection. I have taken every effort to make this book as complete and accurate as possible. I am only human and there may be some differences in perception and interpretation.

I eliminated most of the names of supervisory personnel so that any mention of them will not be interpreted in any negative manner or appear libelous to any company personnel.

This book wasn't written to cast judgment on who was right or who was wrong, it was written to show the public my life as a steel worker: my loves, hates, pain, my everyday experiences while working in a steel plant. I wrote the book to be not only informative but also entertaining.

David Kuchta

The plant between 1907 and 1920.

BETHLEHEM STEEL
A BRIEF HISTORY

THE LEHIGH VALLEY has a long history of ironmaking. From 1840, when the first anthracite-fueled blast furnace was successfully blown in at Biery's Bridge (Catasauqua), to 1995, when Bethlehem Steel shut down the "hot end" of its Bethlehem plant, ironmaking has been an integral part of the local economy.

The story of Bethlehem Steel begins in 1857 when Bethlehem merchant Augustus Wolle became interested in developing large iron deposits near Hellertown and building furnaces nearby. One of the initial stockholders in his Saucona Iron Company was the principal stockholder and virtual ruler of the Lehigh Valley Railroad, Asa Packer.

Packer directed Robert H. Sayre, the general superintendent and chief engineer of the Lehigh Valley Railroad, to take an active role in the affairs of the new company. Sayre used the railroad's financial resources to take control of the Saucona Iron Company, which was reorganized in 1858 as the Bethlehem Rolling Mill and Iron Company. The site selected for the plant was the junction of the Lehigh Valley and North Pennsylvania railroads.

The railroad badly needed a source of high-quality iron rails. In one of their first actions, the board of managers hired John Fritz as ironmaster. Fritz was a mechanical genius. He had recently invented a "three-high" mill for rolling rails by passing the hot blooms rapidly back and forth through the rolls. In conventional "two-high" mills, the hot blooms could not be completely rolled into rails in a single operation, because they had to be dragged to the front of the mill after each pass through the rolls. They cooled during the process and would often crack or shatter while being rolled.

By the time the first furnace was erected and the first cast made in January of 1863, the company's name had been changed to the Bethlehem Iron Company. The first rails were rolled in September of that year, and quickly gained a reputation for excellence. The Lehigh Valley Railroad bought most of the initial production; the Central Railroad of New Jersey also became a major customer.

While the Bethlehem Iron Company's plant was being developed, Bessemer steel rails were becoming increasingly available. Imported from England, they were far more costly but lasted many times longer than iron rails. Urged on by the Lehigh Valley Railroad's need for rails of the highest quality, Fritz designed steelmaking facilities for the Bethlehem Iron Company. Fritz had designed the Bessemer steel plant as an integrated unit, with rolling mills for rails and merchant bar stock adjacent to the Bessemer converters. Within a year of its completion in 1873 the new plant had established a national reputation both for its productivity and for the quality of its rails.

By 1881 the company had six large anthracite-fueled furnaces in South Bethlehem. But by this time, coke-fueled furnaces in the Pittsburgh region were beginning to dominate the iron industry and the rail market.

The Bethlehem Iron Company moved to heavy forgings as its specialty product during the 1880s. The first battery of basic open hearth furnaces was fully operational by 1888. By 1892 the company had the finest steel forging equipment in the world, capable of producing armor plate and cannon of almost any size. It received lucrative government contracts for guns and armor plate.

The U.S. warships that won the great naval victories of the 1898 Spanish American War were largely equipped with ordnance, armor plate, and machinery parts made in Bethlehem. The company also produced engine forgings for ocean liners, field rings for the generators in the new Niagara Falls hydroelectric plant, and the axle for the famed 246-foot-high Ferris wheel that was the centerpiece of the 1892-93 Chicago World's Fair. This axle, 45½ feet long and weighing over 56 tons, was the largest steel forging made to that date.

In 1901 the Bethlehem Steel Company, under Charles M. Schwab (1862-1939), took over the facilities of the Bethlehem Iron Company. Schwab was among the most brilliant and innovative steelmakers in America. As the personal protégé of Andrew Carnegie, he had risen to become president of Carnegie Steel, and had personally negotiated the merger of Carnegie Steel with the steel interests of J.P. Morgan to create the United States Steel Corporation, of which he became the first president. Schwab's flamboyant management and personal lifestyle clashed with the more conservative outlook of U.S. Steel's chairman, Elbert Gary, and Schwab resigned from the corporation that he had done much to create. In 1904, as president of the Bethlehem Steel Company, he combined Bethlehem with the remains of the bankrupt United States Shipbuilding Company to create the Bethlehem Steel Corporation.

Schwab possessed an intimate knowledge of U.S. Steel's strengths and weaknesses. During the first decade of his ownership of Bethlehem Steel, he counterprogrammed its expansion to exploit chinks in his larger competitor's armor. He installed a crucible steel plant since U.S. Steel did not own such a facility, built an open hearth rail mill that produced products superior to the Bessemer steel rails produced by U.S. Steel, and added a drop forging plant since U.S. Steel was not willing to enter this market.

Schwab's boldest decision was to enter the growing but fiercely competitive structural steel market in 1905 with the installation of a Grey mill to produce continuously rolled wide flange beams. This mill, invented by immigrant British engineer, Henry Grey (1846-1913), rolled wide flange beams directly from ingots. These beams were wider, stronger, less likely to bend—and cheaper to produce—than conventional beams. Since they were continuously rolled as a single section, they eliminated the high costs of riveting and other fabrication. By July 1908 the Saucon Division, containing a Grey mill and open hearth furnaces, was placed in operation under the leadership of Eugene Grace (1876-1960), who became Schwab's chief protégé and eventual successor as head of Bethlehem Steel.

The workforce of the Bethlehem Iron Company was initially composed of local residents who were primarily of Germanic ancestry. By the 1890s significant numbers of Irish and immigrants from eastern and southern European countries found employment at the ever-expanding plant. By the first decade of the twentieth century the workers of the Bethlehem Steel Corporation were of many nationalities. Many of them lived in South Bethlehem, near the plant. Major shopping areas on Third and Fourth streets grew up to serve their needs. In those prosperous years, immigration to South Bethlehem from central, southern, and eastern Europe reached the proportions of a flood. Many came from the polyglot Austro-Hungarian Empire, including Austrians, Hungarians, Slovaks, Slovenes (Windish), and Ruthenians. Poles and Ukrainians also found work at Bethlehem, as did Italians, who probably formed one of the largest immigrant groups in South Bethlehem, coming mainly from central and northern Italy. Greeks also migrated to South Bethlehem, while Jews came to the community to set up stores. Other ethnic communities, such as Romanians, also became visible in South Bethlehem.

These ethnic groups tended to cluster together in various departments of the great steel plant. One department might be composed entirely of Hungarians, while another might be made up entirely of

Slovenes. This was made more pronounced by plant foremen, who had the power to hire and fire within their shops.

In general, Bethlehem Steel was spared the labor unrest that plagued other steel companies until 1910, when a long and violent strike occurred over the issue of forced overtime work. Using the power of the company's economic muscle, aided by the Pennsylvania State Police, Charles Schwab was able to emerge victorious.

The outbreak of World War I in 1914 proved to be a bonanza for the Bethlehem Steel Corporation. By the end of that year Bethlehem Steel had received over $200 million in orders from Britain and France and embarked on rapid expansion of its production facilities. In 1913 the plant had a workforce of 9,000 men, while by 1915 this number had swelled to 24,567 employees, of whom more than 2,000 were employed on plant construction alone. After the United States entered the war in 1917, the company underwent a further expansion and its workforce totalled more than 35,000, many of whom were women. Workers from Mexico also found jobs at the plant during this period. Between April of 1918 and the the ceasefire in November, Bethlehem was the largest and most important munitions and ordnance manufacturer serving the Allied cause. In order to achieve this miracle of productivity, the company had expended more than $102 million for new facilities.

The enormous profits earned by the Bethlehem Steel Corporation during World War I enabled its management to finance the acquisition of many of the remaining American steelmakers, beginning in 1916 with the purchase of the Pennsylvania Steel Company and its subsidiary, the Maryland Steel Company. This gave Bethlehem large plants at Steelton, Pennsylvania, and Sparrows Point, Maryland. In 1919 Bethlehem gained control of the Cambria Steel Company of Johnstown, Pennsylvania. This buying spree culminated in 1922 with the purchase of the Lackawanna Steel Company, which operated a large plant near Buffalo, New York.

Bethlehem Steel prospered greatly during the building boom of the 1920s. However, the Great Depression, which began in 1929, brought hard times and not until the deteriorating world situation of the late 1930s forced the United States to begin a rearmament program did prosperity return. As the pace of rearmament increased, Bethlehem became the target of a violent strike in 1941 that resulted in the company's recognition of the United Steelworkers of America as the bargaining agent for its workers.

When World War II broke out in 1939 the Bethlehem plant once again entered a period of great prosperity. By 1943 over 33,000 workers, among them great numbers of women, were employed at the Bethlehem plant. Peak production of armor plate ordnance and munitions was reached during October of 1944 when one million 75mm and 90mm shells, 732,000 rough shell forgings, and 21,200 tons of gun forgings and finished guns were produced. The drop forge facility during World War II manufactured an incredible 83 percent of America's total production of aircraft engine cylinders.

During the 1950s the facilities of the Bethlehem plant continued to be upgraded and after a series of lengthy strikes workers gained better pay and benefits. The Bethlehem plant provided employment opportunities not only for thousands of residents of the Lehigh Valley but also for thousands of unemployed miners and coal-region youth after the collapse of the anthracite-mining industry.

By the 1960s long-term trends began to become evident that would eventually threaten the survival of the Bethlehem plant. The most important of these was the construction of the greenfield Burns Harbor plant on Lake Michigan. By the end of the decade this new facility had become the corporation's major profit center. Ordnance production at Bethlehem ceased in 1968, and with the exception of a minor revival in 1987-89, Bethlehem no longer produced the products that once made it world famous.

Beginning in the 1970s and accelerating in the 1980s the Bethlehem plant's workforce began to shrink as department after department was deemed to be unprofitable and closed. Drop forge, steel fabrication, tool steel and other departments vanished. Finally, on November 18, 1995, steel production ceased at the Bethlehem plant. Where once more than 30,000 workers had labored, fewer than 2,000 remain in a truncated plant that is for sale.

It is through the memories of individuals such as David Kuchta that the skills, trials, and high jinks that characterized the daily lives of the workers can be retrieved and preserved for future generations. Kuchta's *Memoirs of a Steelworker* will give all who read it insights into a now-vanished working man's culture.

Lance Metz
Historian, Hugh Moore Historical Park and Museums

"A" Furnace in 1995   Joseph Elliott

INTRODUCTION

THIS BOOK IS WRITTEN about my forty years of work at the Bethlehem Steel Company's plant in Bethlehem, Pennsylvania. My career started in August of 1952 and ended in 1992. The information obtained throughout the years was all on-site observations and experiences. It is not what management would like you to believe, but what really happened and how it happened. It's what happened behind the scenes. It's actually the inner workings of a Super Giant. This is a story about what happened every day. It's information that no one talked about, no less wrote about.

I could honestly say that I worked on or in every building in the six-mile-long plant.

The story is not only my autobiography as I remember it, but the biography of every steel worker that ever worked for the Bethlehem Steel Company. At times it is also the autobiography of the plant itself, because I do write as if the company and myself are one.

Many of the blue collar workers of the Bethlehem plant had wives who worked throughout the main or corporation offices. What this did was give many of us workers an inside pipeline of projects or long-term plans that the company had intentions of doing.

Yes, many of us workers had the inside track to this information far in advance, before our own supervision knew anything.

When I was writing this book, the memories flowed. The biggest and saddest part was my memories of watching this plant slowly deteriorate. There were times that the corporation breathed new life into the mother plant, only to watch it go down the tubes once again.

Through the last 20 years, the workers had the feeling that top management wanted to shut down the Bethlehem plant. This did have a bad effect on much of the work force. Many workers felt discouraged when they heard the management of Bethlehem Steel talking about shutdowns. Many thought, "why the hell should I give the company my best, when they don't care." It did seem as if there was a goal, to close down the matriarch of the Bethlehem Steel Corporation.

It is sad because almost always through the years and even when times were bad, the Bethlehem plant always seemed to show a profit on its operation. It wasn't until recent years, when the company took huge write-offs, when they closed down sections of the Bethlehem plant's operations, that it showed a loss. Yes, it was only a paper loss.

I remember when the Sparrows Point plant was operating in the red. The Bethlehem plant held its head high above the turbulent waters. The Bethlehem plant helped the corporation survive.

Plant managers or supervisors that came to the Bethlehem plant from other plants of the Bethlehem Corporation complained about the workers from other plants. They claimed that on pay days, Friday or Monday, how many of these workers reported off. They also mentioned how impressed they were with the calibre of the workers here at the Bethlehem plant. When I heard this kind of remark it did make me feel special and feel proud of the Bethlehem plant.

Year after year, the rolling mills in the Bethlehem plant broke their own production records. Breaking past production records was done on old, obsolete equipment and machinery. It truly was amazing. In the end all this performance and production records meant nothing.

The old mills were held together with workers' ingenuity. They kept this antiquated equipment operating through the worst of conditions. The crews that operated and maintained it were dedicated workers. They had that certain something that the newer generation lacks.

The top management of the corporation looked at the "Grand Old Matriarch" of the Bethlehem Steel Corporation as an old, rusting, antiquated plant. They failed to see her as the Grand Old Matriarch that helped build the corporation into what it is today. Through the profits of the Bethlehem plant, the other plants came into being.

Management failed to remember that it was <u>she</u> who made <u>them</u>. Some of these very top management people failed to remember that they were helped with their education and training by her. They also didn't remember that many production records were made by this grand old lady of the steel industries.

In the end, she reached out for help, but no one cared. It did seem that this Bethlehem plant with its bad location was not supposed to become the Number Two Giant in the steelmaking industry.

Because of its location, she was written off. This grand old lady, the mother of the Bethlehem Steel Corporation, didn't deserve the unbecoming end that is happening to her right now as I am writing this book. She is slowly but methodically being shut down and scrapped piece by piece.

Most of the Lehigh part of the plant from Fahy Bridge up to the Minsi Trail Bridge was sold for two million dollars with the stipulation that the company will buy all the scrap steel for twenty dollars under the going scrap price. God, what a waste!

First they cut off the toe, then the foot, and then the leg. Now they are removing the very heart and soul of this Grand Old Lady of the steel industries.

The blue collar workers did everything possible to save her, they cooperated in every manner to do whatever was possible to keep the plant in operation (without losing face), but it is my opinion that the plant was written off by management many years ago. My opinion is that management probably thought it had lasted too long as far as they were concerned.

When I started writing my memoirs in the fall of '95, the prospects of the Steel surviving didn't look very promising. Conditions have progressed downhill ever since.

It was a sad day for the workers, the city of Bethlehem, and the whole Lehigh Valley when they shut down the hot end of the plant and silenced the 48-59-inch mill in 1995. It was even sadder when they announced in late 1996 that the combo mill, the press forge and everything else that's still operating, except Martin Tower, the plant railroad and the cokeworks, was for sale.

I feel nothing but sadness to have to say goodbye to a large part of my life. Sure, I'm retired, but the Steel is still a part of me. It's just like being an alumnus of certain colleges and universities. I also feel a certain compassion for my remaining Union brothers who will lose their jobs.

When the Steel is gone, the graves of the hundreds of fallen workers will remain. I do hope these workers will not be forgotten, for they gave their lives so the Corporation could prosper and grow. Management probably wrote them off long ago. Usually when a worker died from any type of accident, it was considered his fault. It was never the company's fault. These workers gave the ultimate that any worker can possibly ever give to a company. I imagine that many of these workers who are buried on hills overlooking the Steel Company would have tears in their eyes if they could see what is happening to their beloved steel plant.

This book is my way of saying goodbye to a Grand Old Lady of the steel industry. It is also my tribute to the working men of the Bethlehem plant who made her as great as she was.

Joseph Elliott

Bending press in the Weldment Shop. Still in use, this is an original Whitworth press installed during the 1886-1892 expansion of the plant.

GETTING HIRED:

FIRST JOB, WELDMENT

MY CAREER OF FORTY YEARS with the Bethlehem Steel Company started in August of 1952. Upon graduation from Lansford High School I set my goals at taking a short vacation and then heading down to the employment office of the Bethlehem Steel Company. These offices were located in a basement of the Steel's plant office.

Since the Korean War was in effect, the Steel had many government contracts and were looking for additional employees. At the time of my graduation the steel workers were out on strike from April 29 up to July 24. The strike lasted a total of 53 days.

The demand for manpower throughout the Lehigh Valley was so great that the steel company couldn't get enough able-bodied personnel from the valley itself, so they were running full-page newspaper ads for workers all through the coal region area.

They needed all types of skilled workers, from welders to machine operators, but what they needed most were people without degrees or skills, people with strong backs and the willingness to work and to do what was asked of them without asking why.

1951 and 1952 were the first major years that the steel company hired Puerto Ricans, right from Puerto Rico. Many didn't even speak English. The Steel was desperate for laborers for their CSL (Construction and Labor) labor gang, chippers for the Ingot Mould Foundry, and for people to work the coke ovens at the Coke Work Division.

In those days there weren't too many tests that potential workers had to take. A major physical, and just filling out standard employment forms was about all you needed to do.

After I filled out the necessary forms, I went to an interviewer who made the decision on what department they would place me in.

When he interviewed me, he saw that I was from the coal regions. He asked to look at my hands. Yes, he was disappointed. They weren't calloused and beat up from picking coal. He thought that the CSL or the Coke Works wasn't the place to send me. He said that I was going to work in a place called Weldment and that they were making tanks at that time.

My first thought was that these tanks had to be Army tanks. What a disappointment! They were large cylindrical tanks used for storage of propane and other types of gas. Thinking back, these tanks were really put together. I would imagine they are still being used today.

My first department symbol and number was DL 214.

My very first job was sweeping the floors of the shop. Cleaning up slag from the burning and layout tables and putting away what seemed like tons of welding rods. Sweeping the floors was a monotonous job. I really hated it. It was a very boring job. The floors of the various bays of Weldment were immaculate. In fact, it was hard finding a place to look busy.

When I first started working in Weldment, I remember seeing a fellow laborer who was sweeping up the floors with a push broom fall fast asleep, standing up. I found out that he worked a full shift at Bethlehem Steel, and a full shift at Mack Trucks. He also worked at a fruit stand in Allentown in his spare time and on weekends.

I remember one day while sweeping dust, our shop superintendent took his daily walk through he shop. When he saw me sweeping next to nothing he became quite upset. Hell, it wasn't my fault. I had already cleaned everything that needed cleaning.

Weldment's superintendent was a small, balding man by the name of Louie Fine. In those days, superintendents were treated like gods. He tried to give the impression that he was tough and mean. He would walk around the shop with both his hands folded behind his back with a slight bent-over posture. At work, he kept up the image of tough and mean but at home he was a regular guy who fixed all the kids' bikes in the neighborhood.

In those days, there was no sitting around and waiting for some job to crop up. They wanted you on the move at all times.

Here is a little embarrassing story about what happened to me. One day I had a terrific toothache. I went around the shop looking for some aspirin. Nobody had any. One of the welders, who chewed tobacco, suggested that chewing tobacco will kill the pain. I was desperate so took a good mouthful of chew. What a mistake. I got sick like a dog. I got so sick that I went into our welfare room and lay down. Someone told the superintendent that I was sick and lying down on the bench. When he came in and found out that I was sick from chewing tobacco, he hollered out, get him the hell out of here, what do you think we are running, a Kindergarten school? I was so sick, that I thought to myself, go to hell you little bastard, and just kept lying there. After about an hour I felt better and went back to work. A little green around the gills, that's for sure. Some of these things we never forget.

Whenever someone went on vacation or reported off sick, I would fill in as chainman or grinder. Since these jobs paid 10 to 15 cents an hour more, I relished the idea of getting them. I personally liked keeping busy. I wasn't afraid of work. But in the same instance, if there is nothing to do, then I would rather sit down and relax. I never liked the idea of pretending to be busy. You were busy or you weren't.

In time I was promoted to chainman and then to grinder. At that time they were starting welding classes. I finally was in line to go to welding school when the bottom dropped out. The Korean War ended, and work slacked off. I was put back on the broom and then put on loan slip to the dreaded CSL labor gang.

Loan Slip to the Labor Gang

This was the worst work in the whole steel company except for working on top of the coke ovens in the Coke Works or being a chipper at the Ingot Mould Foundry. Many of these chippers down through the years ended up with silicosis.

I was in my early twenties and found out no matter what they threw at me in this labor department, I could take it. The supervision in the labor gang were known to be tyrants. They treated their workers like we were all a bunch of uneducated dummies. They resented you if you asked them, "why?" After a while most adapted to their ways and did what was asked of them. The CSL Department had a way of breaking the spirit of its workers.

What we did do in the CSL Department was a lot of hot work on open hearth rebuilds. It seemed like this type of work was an ongoing thing. We never caught up. As soon as one furnace was done, another went down. We also did all the dirty work of removing all the brick from the stack of the blast furnaces when they went down for rebuilds. The air in the blast furnace stack was potent. Ammonia burned your eyes. One thing it did do, if your nose was blocked, it sure opened it up fast.

At this time, remodeling of the beam yards was taking place. As laborers we would do the pick-and-shovel work and also stripped a lot of forms from the new concrete piers and foundations. The laborers were also in charge of pouring all the concrete in these jobs. Some days we poured concrete the whole eight-hour shift.

(Above) Tapping an open hearth furnace into a teeming ladle at No. 4 Open Hearth in the Saucon Division. This is an early photograph, before the days of mandatory hard hats and safety glasses.

(Below left) No. 2 Open Hearth (Saucon) in 1915. (Below right) Teeming ingots at No. 1 or No. 3 Open Hearth. Molten steel is being poured (teemed) from the ladle into ingots. The "observer" is using an instrument to check the temperature; the ladle operator and the steel pourer are to his right.

Another job we had to do was go under some of the existing hot beds and clean scale and grease. The old beds were low. You seemed to be bent over all day long. This was truly a God-forsaken job.

Another job that was tough was pool labor work. Many of the old laborers liked this job, because it paid a better piece-rate bonus. Bent over for eight hours in a railroad car, throwing out chunks of chrome ore that were very heavy, didn't seem like my cup of tea. This was more like slave labor or something a chain gang would do.

In time I saw a lot of other loan slip workers get called back to their shops. I just waited and waited, but my call never came.

Working on the rebuilds of open hearths or certain pre-heating furnaces is a job you never forget. I think that if there is a hell on this earth, this must have been it.

Chipping Checkers and Cleaning out Flues

Some of the jobs on the open hearth furnace rebuilds were like coming face to face with hell itself. The heat at times was unbearable. I remember one time when one of the workers brought in a thermometer that went up to 150 degrees. The temperature went up and up until it hit the 150 degree mark and broke. That's hot!

No, I'm not overstating the heat conditions. Some of the places I worked at times glowed red a few feet from where I worked. When I removed a layer of firebrick or slag, the bricks behind it were red.

Top of the list of the worst jobs were two jobs called chipping checkers and cleaning out the flues. For some reason the leader of our crew that I worked for was always selected for this type of work. It could be that many of us were from the coal regions or from the farm areas.

This work area was beneath the furnace and was located on both the east and west ends of what is called the pan or hearth. They were air chambers where hot gases and air were recirculated or vented into the stack area. When these furnaces went down for rebuilds, we would get all the tools and equipment we needed. We then would go there and break in the seal.

Picture this: It looked like a large brick oven with a vertical brick wall at one end. We would break through this wall and remove all the brick. When we got our first glimpse inside, everything was pure red. We would then place two or three large fans in front of the opening. These fans also provided the air we breathed. Without these fans, it would have been impossible to breathe at all. We would hose down the bricks with water hoses. This made an immense cloud of steam! After a few hours, the red glow would turn black. Believe me, it was still as hot as blazes.

The floor of the chamber was bricks stacked in a fashion that was called checkering. This is where the name "checkers" came from. The hot air, gases and dirt went down through the openings in these bricks into a chamber below called the flues. More on this later.

Hot slag would accumulate over and inside these openings in the bricks. Dirt would also accumulate in the openings. Because of this the openings in the bricks would get smaller or close up completely, preventing the hot air or gases from circulating properly. Our job was to go in there and with a four- or five-foot bar we had to jab, poke, or chip at these openings until they opened up.

This doesn't sound too bad, does it? Believe me, it was a living hell!

We would have three or four crews of workers that would work in spells. While one crew was inside chipping at the bricks, we would just sit and wait. Just sitting there in anticipation of what was ahead drained one's enthusiasm. When it was our turn to go in and chip, we would have to put on a full-length furnace overcoat. We put on leggings, heavy asbestos gloves and a dust shield over our head and face. We would also put on a pair of wooden shoes. These were wooden soles with straps. If we didn't wear them the rubber on the soles of our shoes would melt. Before the rubber melted, any nails in the soles or heels would heat up to a point were they burned our feet.

One furnace was so hot that we timed the length of the time one of the other crews stayed in and chipped: a total of 45 seconds. It took five or more minutes to put on all the protective clothing and the crew spent less than one minute working.

When my buddy and I went in we stayed for at least three or four minutes. There was a reason for this. My buddy was a fellow who lived on a farm near Lehighton. He was definitely from the old school and believed hard work would never kill anyone. He gave it his all and didn't hold back. Don't ask me why, but Steve and I would stay in the longest or fill more buckets of flue dirt than anyone else. I think it had to do with being "macho." It sure didn't have anything to do with money. The laborer's salary was the lowest in the plant, besides the janitor's.

When I think back, maybe we worked like this for pride. Pride in accomplishment. I don't know. Young people in this day and age would say that we were crazy.

To give you an idea of just how much heat was in these areas we worked, whenever our belt buckles went against our bare skin, the skin got burned. At that time our safety glasses had metal frames. The frames of the glasses burned our face. I kid you not, it was really hot!

Whenever we finished our stint at chipping at the brick checkers with the large bar, the bars got so hot that they were literally thrown out of the openings. It is amazing that no one ever got hit or speared with these bars. There were some close calls. Because of these difficult working conditions, tempers flared.

When it was time to work in the flue area, we had to climb down a ladder to get into them. This was the lowest area of the open hearths. I felt like I was working in a cave. A stinking hot cave. In most flues, we had to stay bent over while we shoveled flue dirt into a large metal drum. We put the filled drum or bucket on a metal roller line and pushed it toward the openings where someone else hoisted it up to the floor above. Most of the time, when conditions were extra hot, most crews would fill only three or four drums. Working with my over-ambitious buddy, we usually sent one extra bucket more than anyone else.

The flues had no air and were as hot as hell. At times, steam agitators were stuck in an open position and steam blew out of them continuously. I remember one time when we were down in the flues and someone closed the large metal and brick damper door that shut off the air from flowing up the stack. The only way we could get enough air to breathe was through the draft created by the tall stacks.

When the door shut, all the remaining air became unbearably hot and we couldn't even breathe. We literally flew up the ladder to the safety of the floor above. My work clothes were so hot that when I brushed my hand against them, I burned myself. Now that's hot!

The icing on the cake was when our supervisors would ask us to work a double shift during the winter months. We would be working in these hot areas and every inch of our clothing would be soaked to the skin with sweat. Instead of leaving us at that job, they would send us outside in a freezing cold, windy snowstorm to clean, salt and cinder walkways. It was amazing that none of us ever caught pneumonia.

The job on the CSL labor gang was so bad that hundreds of men would be hired, only to quit after a week or so. Many workers would quit the very first day on the job. Most thought that this was no job befitting man nor beast, but to some of us, it was a job. What kept most of the guys that I worked with working, was the anticipation of returning back to our old shops in the steel company where we were laid off from originally. When we eventually went back to our old departments or got transferred to other jobs, it was like dying and going to heaven. What a difference.

The open hearths at the Bethlehem plant are no longer in operation. Most workers were happy to see them go. For me, I have my memories. Some memories are not so great, but memories nevertheless.

CSL Laborers

The laborers weren't treated fairly compared to other workers in the plant. I remember one instance where our crew was given a job raking and sprucing up an open area around one of the offices. This was considered easy work, good work. No one killed themselves as far as the work went, but you had to keep busy. Eight hours of this was boring and tiring. If you stood around too long, someone in the nearby office would call the labor office and complain to our bosses that we were goofing off. No one ever had any compassion for the CSL laborer.

The next day the field foreman explained to our crew that he gave us a good easy job and he sort of expected us to work a little harder and not complain about the crummy job we were about to get. Yes indeed, work in those earlier years was not that great.

I remember working the old 12- and 18-inch pre-heating billet furnace. When you worked in that furnace you were bent over. The worst part of this was that the slag and scale would be built up so bad, that you literally worked on your hands and knees. Remember, the slag and scale were very hot.

Many times we had to use large jackhammer-type busters to break up the slag. You operated these jackhammers while bent over. The floor of these furnaces was so hot that we had to wear wooden shoes. Even with these wooden shoes our feet would burn. The clincher was that on the low ceiling of these furnaces were small three- to four-inch stalactites formed by melting slag that accumulated on the ceiling. Whenever you forgot yourself and tried to straighten up, you would jab your back or head on one of these little devils. These furnaces were living hell.

In later years they rebuilt them and made the ceilings of the furnaces a little higher. But just like everything that is done to make conditions better at the steel, it seems that in a short time, they were shut down and demolished.

I have told you about all the bad things of working hot jobs, now let me tell you the rewarding part. You received a full ten cents an hour more for hot work. How about that!

CSL — Final Days

When you worked for the CSL Department, labor and construction, the whole rest of the plant looked at you as low life. Yes, everyone thought that if you were dumb enough to work for that particular outfit you couldn't have any brains. It was that bad. Instead of a little compassion or understanding, our own union brothers had contempt.

I remember working on stripping some forms in a small pit down at the beam yards. A couple of beam-yard workers passed by and one of them made the following comment; "They look like a bunch of rats in a hole." At that point it took everything I had to hold back from going after him to make him eat those words. It was bad enough that our own self-esteem was at an all-time low, without some smart ass making comments like that.

Many men took this job because they needed work. They took this job hoping that something better might come along.

In the fifties and sixties, if you wanted to get out of the CSL Department, you had to quit. You had to terminate your job and then try to get rehired in one of the other shops. Some were lucky. I myself didn't get called back to my old shop, Weldment, and I wanted out. As bad as it was, I wouldn't quit. I'm no quitter.

Through a friend of mine that I worked with in Weldment and then in the labor gang, he helped me get out. He got me a transfer to another department. This fellow was taking courses at Lehigh University. He graduated and then got a supervisor-type job with the Labor Construction Department, no less. He got on as a safety supervisor. He did try to get me into the Rigger Department, but with my luck, they stopped hiring at that time.

The new shop that I was going to go to was the Carpenter Department or CSC, which later got the symbol number 405. I also would hold my seniority. It was a few years later that plant seniority came into effect. Before this it was all shop seniority. When this happened, many of the old CSL laborers bidded out of that hell hole and got into better departments that had much better working conditions and also better pay scales. They had a chance to go up the ladder. When this changeover took effect, not too many of the young plant workers were too happy.

What happened is that the old CSL workers had a lot of company time and when they went to their new jobs, this seniority went along with them. They automatically had more seniority than many of the original workers in that particular shop. When openings came for better positions and higher-paying jobs, these new (old-timers) were in line for these jobs. These old CSL laborers paid their dues; believe me they deserved something better. Besides, most all companies have plant seniority. The shop seniority was a throwback from years past.

When I got out of the laborers, I was one happy guy.

Looking northeast from the roof of the Roll Shop. The Carpenter Shop is in the foreground, with the soaking pits beyond.

Joseph Elliott

CARPENTERS CSC (405)

IN 1956, I RECEIVED MY TRANSFER to the carpenter department. My symbol and number at that time was CSC 156 and then later became 405 – 152. In the earlier years all departments were designated by letters, which were later changed to numbers.

My first job was doing labor-type work. We cleaned the roofs and gutters of all the buildings in the Bethlehem plant and we also cleaned the roofs in preparation for roof-coating jobs. As laborers we pulled different materials up to the roof area, such as roofing paper, sheet iron and insulation. In later years they did away with the carpenter laborers and regular-rated carpenters had to do this same work that we did as laborers.

We did everything the old-fashioned way by using a large pulley with heavy rope. Many times we did this job for an entire eight-hour shift. When I think back about this, the carpenters did nothing but bull work. Carpenters were the last department to get modernized. Many of the workers throughout the plant said that we worked like they did it in the cave man days. At times, I think they were right.

In later years we would beg, borrow or steal the use of the riggers' Pettibone crane to put up piles of sheet iron on the roofs, where we were working. This certainly made things better and easier and it also saved our backs.

Carpenters' Various Jobs

The carpenters did a large diversity of jobs. There was the regular carpenter type of work that one expects from a carpenter, such as fixing or replacing windows and doors. We did a lot of office remodeling such as putting in new hardwood floors, paneling, or ceiling tiles. Our carpenters had a large carpenter shop that had all the equipment needed to make anything out of wood. There also was a section for the tin smiths who made all the roof flashings and the air conditioning duct work. They also metalclad most of the doors in the plant.

Most of the shop carpenters were hand selected and they worked in the shop full time. They were considered shop carpenters. All the rest of us were called field carpenters. We did a large variety of work from building wood frame buildings to railroad car blocking.

Most of all the scaffold work was done by plant carpenters. All shops had the right to put up any scaffold up to 12 feet high. Larger than that they had to call in the plant carpenters.

When bricklayers needed any scaffold, they called in the carpenters. We built every scaffold for them from the small three-foot buck scaffold to massive pipe scaffolds for larger buildings. This also included all furnace scaffolds.

One thing about the bricklayers was that most of them were like a bunch of babies when it came to building them a scaffold. Everything had to be just right. If an opening in the planks was bigger than an inch, they would insist on us replanking or filling in the gaps. For some reason, they would make sure that whenever there was a scaffold change, they got a long lunch break out of it. I don't know how they did this, but it happened all the time.

The heaviest scaffolds were the front wall scaffold of the open hearth furnaces. This was all heavy bull work. The front wall scaffolds ran the full length of the open hearth furnace and were about five feet wide. We tripled the safety plank on these scaffolds. This was done because the bricklayers would put several pallets of fire brick or carbon brick on the scaffold at the same time. They really loaded it down, from one end to the other. The bricklayers were noted for this. They constantly overloaded all the scaffolds. Thank God, no one ever got hurt with a scaffold collapsing.

The scaffold planks were two or more inches thick, and were from 16 feet to 22 or more feet long and heavy as hell. They were Oregon pine, still green and full of sap. These scaffolds were built above the charging doors so all the plank had to be lifted and pushed into place. This was hard work and it seemed to be one of the jobs that I got stuck with, quite often.

We also put in all the roof centers for the bricklayers to lay the fire brick that made the main roof of the furnace. These centers were heavy and took at least four carpenters to put them in place. I also got elected for that job. It's amazing I don't have real bad back problems!

Another job we did big-time in the plant was building all the forms for pouring cement. We did all types of form work, from building them from scratch to installing factory-made panels. We also installed all the anchor bolts for fastening down the machinery.

In the early years, the carpenters installed all the reinforcement rods for the concrete jobs. In later years the riggers took over this job. I did enjoy this type of work when I was a rigger, but it got very hard on my back and knees as I aged.

Some of the acres of roofs in the Bethlehem plant. This is looking over the Beth-Forge No. 2 Treatment Shop (on the right) from the top of No. 3 High House. On the left is part of Weldment. The building with the high monitors is John Fritz's original forge shop.

Carpenters did all the roof work in the steel company. This was from building new roofs to fixing up the old roofs. The company put out on bid many of the big roof jobs to outside contractors. More on this later.

We did a lot of three-ply, built-up roofs, which was hot tar and felt roofing paper. Carpenters did all the patching on sheet iron roofs. We also replaced all the old sheet iron with new sheet iron. I guess we were considered sheet-iron mechanics.

Roof work was done all year long. In the spring it was great working out in the fresh air and sunshine. In the winter we froze and in the summer we roasted. Many a job of replacing a sheet iron roof was done in the middle of summer with hot furnaces operating below us. All the heat, dirt and fumes came up into our faces. At times, these jobs were unbearable, but work went on.

23

Since I did more roof work than other work, I guess I could be considered a roofer. On a nice warm spring day, our shirts would come off. Our foreman didn't allow this but when he was gone, off went the shirts. More times than I could remember, supervision from the shops that we were working on would call our office and squeal on us about working without shirts. Hell would fly, but it went in one ear and out the other.

As a carpenter I did a lot of pipe scaffold work. If it was complicated or a high one, then I was usually on it. I did like this type of work. The pipe scaffold was made out of pipes and clamps. Putting it together was like playing with a giant erector set.

Another job that wasn't so glamorous and was also a back breaker was the installation of oak planks in water or sewer trenches. We used heavy two and three inch thick oak planks. These were to hold the dirt walls of the trenches so that the laborers or pipe fitters wouldn't be caught in a cave-in. This work wasn't only heavy, it was also wet and dirty.

You can see that the Bethlehem Steel plant carpenters had a large variety of jobs.

The CSC or Carpenter Department wasn't much better than working for the laborers. Our supervisors pushed and expected a lot of work out of us carpenters in the early years. I got along with most of my foremen, but I had one problem, and that was a big mouth. I spoke my piece. I always gave my supervisors a fair day's work and many times I went the extra mile.

For some reason, the carpenters were the last to get equipment to make their jobs better or easier. While most of the other labor and construction departments had trucks and lift trucks to carry all their materials, we had two-wheel buggies that we had to load by hand then push for long distances. Many times, we would have a large load of lumber or scaffolding spill when we went over railroad tracks. Believe me, this was aggravating as hell. It is amazing that all the carpenters didn't end up with bad backs.

Carpenters' Ratings

When most workers started with the carpenters they would start as helpers. Then in time they would get a chance to take tests for "C", "B", or an "A" rating. Problem was that the CSC or 405 supervision wouldn't give everybody a chance to take these test. Yes, if you had connections or friends in high places, then there was no problem. It wasn't until years later that the union stepped in and set up some kind of guidelines where we could ask for tests every six months. Even then most of the tests were unfair. They had nothing to do with our actual field carpenter work. I mention the A test again in the chapter on working as a rigger.

Ninety percent of those who passed the "A" test, making the combination storm and screen door, got their ratings by cheating. Some, believe it or not, had a complete door made up in the shop when they took the test. They made the door when they worked on middle or night shift when there weren't any supervisors around.

They would make up all the pieces for the door and then hide them until the day of the test. When they took the test, they got the pieces out and put them together. How convenient! While in the carpenters, I never did get my A rating. Many times, I and other "B" carpenters went out with gangs and would do the same work an A man did, but with less pay. This came out of the mouths of our supervisors when questioned about what the difference was between the ratings: a "B" man should do a little more than a "C" man and an "A" man should do a little more than a "B" man. No one ever explained what "a little more" really was.

Other times when someone was taking a test, some shop workers helped certain people taking the test. Some of the doors weren't exactly perfect or took too many hours to finish, but if they liked you and wanted you to have an "A" rating, you would get it. There was always some kind of tiny blemish or problem.

Supervisors had that power to pass or flunk you. Simple as that.

The Rain List

The CSC was not the best of departments to work for. One thing that I hated was a rain list. No other department had it but the carpenters. If work was a little slack or if they needed extra workers out on a Saturday and they didn't want to pay time-and-a-half for overtime, they would utilize the rain list. The only good thing they did was to send home everyone according to a list. The list was by seniority with the youngest worker going home first. His turn wouldn't come up until every carpenter went through the list.

The one reason I hated this list is because I carpooled. When they sent me home, I had no way to go home. I lived about 45 to 50 miles from the Bethlehem plant. Sometimes I would be lucky enough to call someone coming off the night shift or I would go to the gate asking everyone if there was anyone going to Tamaqua or Lehighton or beyond, to get a ride home. If I couldn't find a way home, I had to stay in Bethlehem and waste a day away. Sometimes I slept an hour or two, read The Morning Call, went window shopping or hung out in a restaurant having something to eat. I wasn't a happy camper, that's for sure.

On one occasion they sent me home and when I got to my car, about 12 drops of rain fell. That was the total accumulation of rain drops to settle on the windshields of the cars in the parking lot. This is where a little hate of one's supervision comes in. I am glad that I kept my cool in those days. I really don't know if I could handle something like that, in this day and age. No other department that I know of had this practice of sending their workers home because of rain. Most had inside jobs lined up for such occasions.

I remember being sent home one time because of rain. The very next day, when the sun was shining, they had me scheduled to work inside for the rest of the week. When I complained, they said the job just came in and had to be done. When I checked with that office, they said they had scheduled this work a couple of weeks ago. I guess we call this a little white lie.

Working in the Billet Yards

Along the line, on one of my layoffs, when I took another job in the steel company, I found another chicken-s—— outfit. This was in 1960. The department was 620 or the Billet Yards. They had an extra-large order of billets to be scarfed. They needed a lot of extra scarfers and they recalled many laid-off workers to work as temporary scarfers. The pay scale was higher than my carpenter rate and also in time I received a good piece rate for work done.

Learning the scarfing trade came naturally to me. I did like it and became an "A" scarfer in 10 days. I was quite proud of this accomplishment.

This department had some tough rules. If you came in late, you didn't automatically get your regular job. You had to fill in. Another thing they stressed is that if you reported off for any reason whatsoever, you had to call in that afternoon to see what your new schedule would be. In later years the union wouldn't tolerate this kind of nonsense.

As I remember, this department expected you to be ready for work at least 10 minutes before starting time. You weren't paid for this 10 minutes but they expected you to be there for any instructions or safety talk.

The first night shift that I worked as a scarfer was a real nightmare. When my coffee break came, they gave us 10 minutes. Then midway through the night they gave you a full 10 minutes to eat, rest or whatever. I think I was halfway through my lunch when they blew the whistle for us guys to get back to work.

To be honest, 10 minutes for lunch was the ruling for Bethlehem Steel. Most of the shops gave at least 20 to 30 minutes for lunch time. We did get paid for this time. Supervision had an hour for lunch but supposedly didn't get paid for this time. They were supposed to stay an extra half to one hour past the workers' quitting time. When I worked middle shift, I would see most of them leaving extra early. When we had time cards, one of the office people would stay behind and punch out everyone's time cards. This was standard practice among many of the office workers.

By 5 A.M. I was weaving down the billets. I couldn't even hold my eyes open. They also wanted us to work until 10 minutes before quitting time. Talk about the longest hour. This had to be it!

Another time when I was laid off, I got a laborer job in this same department. After a couple of months I had enough of their nonsense. I didn't need anyone telling me when to blow my nose or when to go to the toilet, that's for sure.

My regular carpenter job was still slack and I had to use a little strategy in getting the hell out of this department. Enough was enough!

Our welfare room where we changed our clothes and showered was in an old section at the New Street Welfare Room. What we did was hang our clothes on a basket that was connected to a cable and chain. This basket was then pulled up to the ceiling. This setup was better than lockers. If your clothes were wet or damp for any reason, they dried nicely.

The baskets started falling because of the old cables and chains. After almost getting hit with one, I went into

Joseph Elliott

the 620 Department's office and raised holy hell. I demanded that they change all the cables and chains. While I was bitching and moaning, I was also placing applications for every job opening in the plant, regardless of whether I had a right to bid for it or not.

In a very short time they called me into the office and told me that a job as carpenter in the Ingot Mould Foundry was open. Well, I grabbed it, that's for sure. This job lasted a few months and I then was called back to my regular CSC carpenter job.

Ingot Mould Carpenter

The ingot mould carpenter job was a good job, but the foundry at that time was quite dirty and many of its workers were coming down with silicosis.

In those days, they had their old welfare rooms. The floors were hosed down every shift but were still filthy and constantly wet. I remember someone knocking my tee shirt off my basket and it fell on this crummy, wet floor. When I picked it up the tee shirt was all wet and black. Talk about losing one's cool! God, was I mad.

While working in this department, I met a worker who was quite different. He was a big black guy with one fine build. Someone you really wouldn't mess with. I think this guy was also an ordained preacher. He was a nice guy except for one peculiarity. I remember going into one of the showers and it was scalding hot. I had to adjust the secondary valves to get the cold water flowing. These valves felt like they were hammered shut. I then used the mixing valves to get a nice warm shower.

When this black guy came into the shower he became visibly upset that someone had dared change the settings of the valves. It seems that this was his personal shower and since nobody else could stand the scalding hot water, no one else used it. Everyone had to share the remaining showers because there weren't enough to go around. He definitely had a problem. This guy eventually got some kind of a job in the main office. I think his last job was in charge of seeing that other blacks or ethnics got treated fairly, and maybe even their own personal shower. Who knows?

Through the years I met a lot of interesting people. Some had experiences with flying saucers. One fellow was shot through the ear fleeing Easton police.

My mind goes back to a time when I was offered a double shift. I had no transportation to get home, as I lived about 50 miles from the plant. A young carpenter who was also staying said that he would take me home.

After my middle shift was over we walked out to the parking lot, where I saw that he had some type of two seater, red sports car. I think it might have been an MG or some other type of British sports car.

He drove down Route 22 about 90 miles per hour. He then went up Route 100 and I don't think that the speedometer ever went below 70 miles an hour. He passed on curves and the crest of hills. Nothing slowed him down. The more I bitched at him, the faster he went. Talk about putting the fear of God in someone! He sure scared the hell out of me. I think that I aged a few years on that particular trip home, but it was the fastest time that I ever made it home from work.

A few years later I heard that this Bethlehem speedster ended his life in a car accident. I guess it was just a matter of time. I am glad that time wasn't when he took me home. And life goes on.

Carpenters' Playtime: Horseplay and Pranks

In a later section of this book, I write about playtime or horseplay in the riggers. This was done mostly by the younger workers. The following is a prank, or as some would call it horse play, that happened over 30 years ago.

We had a large gang of roofers working on the DE Mills roof. At the time we were applying hot tar on the seams of sheet-iron decking. This roof job was on a building at the corner of New Street that led to the New Street Bridge (now the Fahy Bridge).

We had a water line coming up from the ground for drinking purposes. Where the water came out of the pipe there was a five gallon bucket. We had just finished the job for the day and were about to go back to our shop. One of the guys spotted a fellow carpenter by the name of Toby Clauser walking from the DE Mill Annex. He was just crossing New Street. Toby had the reputation of being a penny pincher. He saved every penny he earned and some say that he still had his first communion money. He was my kind of guy, thrifty.

One of the guys said, let's get Toby with a five gallon bucket of water. I think that most of the gang thought that this was a good idea, so we were all guilty more or less. A guy named Vic got the water bucket and went to the edge of the roof. When I looked over, a few seconds before the water poured out of the bucket, I yelled NO! I was too late.

Luckily, a sergeant of the Bethlehem City police force just walked by. Down went the water, all five gallons. Toby didn't get hit, but a guy that had just finished work, with his street clothes on and waiting for a bus to go home, got the whole bucket of water over his head.

We all took off in every direction. By the time we got back to our shop, our supervisor's phone was ringing off the walls. The plant patrol, the city police, and the department that the guy worked for were all calling. They wanted the guilty culprit real bad. There was royal hell.

Vic did say that he would take the blame, but the whole gang was of the opinion that he shouldn't say anything because his job might be in jeopardy. The next day, each worker was called in and asked what had happened and who had done it. Nobody snitched. Nobody knew anything. After a couple of days, things quieted down.

It was a dumb thing to do. It was done on a lark. But believe me, water-dumping on different guys happened quite a bit. Sometimes it got to be a major water battle.

The company certainly doesn't condone horse play, but it did happen. I am just glad nobody ever got hurt.

Another favorite prank of yesteryear was nailing a person's metal lunch box to the floor.

This was done usually at the end of the shift. The empty lunch can was on the floor. The owner, in a hurry to get to the shower, reaches down and grabs the handle and zap — a handle in his hand, and the rest of the box on the floor! The owner of the lunch box was fit to be tied. Mad would be too gentle of a word to explain his feelings. I think if he caught the guy, he would have clobbered him.

If I'm not mistaken, this happened to a guy named Rehrig. He was a butcher on the outside and he thought he knew who had done this to him. One of his young pigs had died, so he put the carcass of the pig on this guy's car motor. After a couple of days it stank to high heaven. The owner of the car blew his top. It was a never-ending battle, at times.

Another prank or horseplay that happened all over the plant was in the showers, when someone turns his back, someone else would turn the handle of the water mixer to ice cold. This at times took your breath away.

Many a shovel, hammer or broom handle got greased up. This was very annoying, especially if you had just put on a brand new pair of gloves.

There is no place in the workplace for horseplay, but regardless of all the preaching against it, it went on.

PARKING

WHEN I FIRST STARTED working for the Bethlehem Steel Company in 1952, the Lehigh section of the plant had next to no parking lots for the blue collar workers. They did have some, but very little, for their office workers. The higher management executives had some indoor parking and one or two parking lots right across the street from the office buildings.

Through the years, the Bethlehem City Police would supply an officer to stop traffic at a cross walk, to help the Steel's office force cross the street. They supplied an officer in the morning and at quitting time.

The early 7:00 A.M. shifts would get most of the spots that were available on the streets or in any available parking lots. The 8:00 A.M. shift, which was most of the labor and construction and a few other shops, found no parking areas close to the plant.

Most of us had to park up by Lehigh University's old football stadium. People who lived in homes closer to the plant would put chairs or ash cans in their spots in front of their homes. Many a steel worker removed the obstacle and parked there only to come out of work to find their tire flattened or the sides of their cars had scratch marks from someone using a nail down the side of the car. You soon learned not to park in such locations. There were minor skirmishes over parking spots. Some workers came out at 7:30 A.M. If you knew him or his car, you would double park and wait for that spot.

One fellow was double parked for about 15 minutes waiting for the driver to come and pull out. Another driver coming down the street pulled around the double parked car and drove into that spot. The fellow waiting was a big fellow and didn't take it lightly about losing this parking spot. He walked over to the guy and punched him smack in the face. I think this guy learned a valuable lesson. No one had pity on him.

In time the steel company's real estate department started buying up buildings and homes around the main gate. More and more parking lots were made. The company macadamized them and put guard rails between the lot and the sidewalks. Most were landscaped with trees and shrubs. They did do a nice job on their parking lots.

As more lots became available it seemed like there were fewer workers. In later years many of these lots that were more than a block away remained empty. In the mid-eighties, I wanted a space closer to the gate.

My supervisor at that time drove me down to the plant patrol office. He introduced me to one of the head supervisors of the plant patrol. I told him that I would like a parking space a little closer to the gate. He told me, when I get more time in the plant I will be eligible for a closer spot.

At that point I said, I have over 30 years seniority now, how many more years do I need? I caught him off guard, that's for sure. He then said that I would get a parking spot right across from the main office or main gate.

After 30 years with the company, I finally saw where 30 years meant something. It was a great moment.

Parking in Saucon

Back in the fifties, parking in Saucon was not that great either. Once again, the early shift got the best parking. Good parking was at a premium. Anyone coming late found no parking whatsoever. Some would park right in the middle of the roads going into the lots. They would leave the door unlocked. This was for the benefit of anyone who wanted to get out of the lot, but were blocked in by that car. Some of these cars were pushed several times.

After a while, some workers got tired of pushing these same cars every time they got out of work. At times some of these cars got pushed into the guard rails and then the guy who pushed the car put on the headlights. When the late driver got out of work, his battery was dead. I certainly never approved of this, but I do understand.

Another problem of parking in the big Steel lots was that they were just south of the open hearths. At times the open hearths would blow out the flues or stacks and all the dirt, crud, and everything else blew all over your car. They were literally covered with particles of dirt. As I remember, some of this stuff that blew out of the stacks was hot when it left the stacks. This wasn't all that great on your car's paint job.

The Saucon parking lots in those earlier years had no fences around them. When parking there during the night shift, many a battery or tire was stolen off your car. You sort of held your breath when you got to your car in the morning.

In the late sixties, when they built the basic oxygen furnaces they bought up a large section of homes and buildings. They built large parking lots and completely enclosed them with an eight-foot chain-link fence, topped with barbed wire.

Once again, more parking spaces and then fewer jobs. In the early nineties, these lots were half empty. As they shut down the basic oxygen furnaces and the 48-inch mill there will be a lot more empty parking spaces.

(Right) 1961 view at Mechanic Street in Northampton Heights, where the BOF was built later in the 1960s.

(Below) View in 1990 from the top of the BOF looking toward the Coke Works and Hellertown, over almost-empty parking lots.

Craig L. Bartholomew.

Joseph Elliott

View of Bethlehem, looking over the Moravian buildings and the heavily urbanized area surrounding the steel plant.

CARPOOLING FOR 40 YEARS

I GUESS I SHOULD EXPLAIN why in the world some of us up-homers, as we are called, traveled close to 100 miles a day to go to work. Many people ask me why I did it and why didn't I just move down to the Lehigh Valley area.

Most of us, people who travel, just like the area we live in and if I had to do it over again, I would do the same thing that I did for the past 40 years.

John Petro from Summit Hill drove every day to work at the Bethlehem Steel Co. He worked steady middle shift, from 4 P.M. to 12 midnight. He worked full time in No. 6 Machine Shop and also worked in the No. 5 mine in Lansford as a contract miner. He would get home from work about 1:00 A.M. and then get up at five, go into the No. 5 mine, get X amount of coal loaded in mine cars and then go home. He was running coal, so that means when he got a certain quota of coal cars out, he could go home. He also worked in a buddy's garage in his spare time and on weekends.

Yes, a lot of coal crackers moved closer to their jobs. Some just couldn't handle all the traveling in all kinds of weather. The trip took about an hour each way. Many times I would doze off. Other times we would talk about everything under the sun. Many a trip we solved the world's problems. Politics also came into the conversation. When hunting season came, the entire trip was about hunting. If you were a non-hunter, you got bored silly.

There was a certain comradery among those who carpooled. This wasn't with everyone. If someone had problems at home they would be very touchy. Just like a keg of dynamite ready to explode. One wrong word and bang!

There were times when certain members of some car pools became downright belligerent. Crabby as a bastard. Some were ready to do battle with everyone. Some just looked for a reason to argue. Thank goodness this type of problem only happened a couple of times.

Through the years, we also had some car pools that had no smoking. Smokers weren't allowed, or they just had to do without. Some smokers would rather drive by themselves than give up smoking. To me it is amazing that no one can drive for one hour without lighting up. Through the years, I saw where smokers had to light up when we were five minutes from work or five minutes from home. They just insisted on stinking up the vehicles.

There also were car pools, especially on middle shift, that had to have a six-pack of beer on the way home. They nursed on that bottle of beer like a little baby. These drinkers were only a minority. Most car pools wouldn't allow such nonsense.

Back in 1953 we were going home after a middle shift. It was about 12:15, going up a road that was about a lane and a half wide. It was also heavily crowned. We saw two guys blocking the road in a very desolate area. They were waving white sheets or pillow cases. As the driver slowed down, one guy walked down one side of the car, the other guy went down the other side. At this point John Petro, who was the driver, stepped on the gas and dug out. As we went up the road we saw a farmhouse with the lights on. We could see sheets and other laundry hanging on a clothes line.

The following day we saw in the paper that several convicts had broken out of jail.

Back in the fifties and sixties, there was bus service from Lehighton to Bethlehem, strictly for steel workers. If most of my carpoolers were on vacation or on a different shift, I would ride the bus.

In the early fifties, steel workers riding the bus had a little excitement. On the way home the bus was stopped and state troopers entered the bus with machine guns drawn. They searched the bus for a couple of escaped convicts. (No convicts on board.)

Many guys who drove alone would ride in the bus if the weatherman called for snow that day. These guys were called snow birds. The drivers saw this quite often.

One particular day, it started snowing hard. By quitting time there was over a foot of snow on the ground. Traffic was bogged down. As the snow piled up, drifts started forming. It was a mess.

After about an hour, and no bus showed up, I thought I better call up to the Lehighton Depot and see if the bus made it down to Bethlehem. They told me, no buses were running at all. I thought great, now what the hell do I do? When we had snows like this and had our cars with us, we always made it home.

At this point I thought: Do I stay the night, or try to get home? Being stubborn like an old mule, I thought getting home was it.

I went down to the Bethlehem train station and they told me that they had a train heading toward Lehighton. I and several other workers caught that train and headed home.

On the way home the train rammed into a car that was stuck in a snow drift at one of the railroad crossings. The train stopped. No one was hurt but the conductor had to get all the license numbers and other information about this collision. When we finally got to our cars in the bus depot parking lot and then finally home, I was eight hours late.

In later years, when some roads were impassable some of the workers went to our union hall and slept the night. Most were cold and some had to sleep on hard benches or floors.

When I worked as ash man up at the Number 5 Boiler House in the Coke Works, one time the snows got so deep that nobody was on the roads. The snow was blowing so hard, you couldn't see anything. The guard rails were getting buried by drifting snow. I finally got onto Route 248 above Bath, when I finally saw a car ahead of me. I thought, Thank you dear God. I just got behind him and followed his two tail lights. What I do remember, is that he was traveling pretty lively. If he ran off the road I would have ran off the road also. All I could see was two tire ruts in the snow, and two tail lights ahead. This is all I needed. I did get home and in good time. That was amazing!

I am proud to say that no matter how bad the weather was from deep snows, ice storms, and even flooded roads, I always made it home from work the day I worked. I guess I was like an old work horse heading toward the barn. Nothing stopped me!

We carpoolers, in all the years of traveling, missed work only a couple of times in all those years. This was usually because of bad ice storms. In 40 years, I was late only about 5 times. This was because of ice storms, or traffic tie-ups. Many a time, we up-homers made it into work, and workers who lived in the Lehigh Valley didn't make it in.

In the early years the cars used for work weren't usually new cars. Most were older vehicles, and some were pretty beat up. In this day and age, I wouldn't even think of riding in some of those junkers.

One carpooler by the name of Phil Jones, from Ringtown, came one morning with the back of the front seat on the passenger side missing. Some cars had big holes in the floor and you could see the roadway passing below you. Some vehicles had broken heaters during the winter season. One guy had a heater that leaked out heat during the summer. Some guys just wouldn't use the heaters and the guys in the back seat froze.

One guy by the name of Charlie Sands drove down to the main gate of the Lehigh Plant. Since I was going to Saucon I had to drive the car to Saucon and park it. He had a common electric cord with a plug on the end hanging beneath his dashboard. He said that when I wanted to start the car, I had to squeeze the two prongs of the electrical plug. I thought he was joking. Believe me, he wasn't! Some guys didn't want to replace bad batteries. They would park the vehicle on a hill and drift it to start it. Just amazing! Most of these guys were usually dropped from our car pools. Some had such a bad reputation that nobody wanted them in their car pools.

In later years, the cars were much newer and they were kept in better condition.

In 40 years we had a few fender benders. Nothing too serious. We had one accident in 1991. This guy ran a stop sign that had just been erected. The car got demolished, but no one got hurt. His wife came down to pick us up. A couple of hours' delay, but no big deal, except for the car. That car was ready for pension anyway.

There were a couple of fatalities of guys driving back and forth to work. Not too many, thank God. One vehicle with carpoolers from McAdoo and Hazelton had a couple of riders die from carbon monoxide poisoning. When the driver stopped to leave them off, one was dead and the other died shortly after.

Many of the cars in different car pools had bad mufflers or exhaust systems. It was either no time to get them fixed, or no money to get the job done. Many of the times we rode with the car windows cracked open in the winter months. Sometimes our eyes would burn because of the bad exhausts. It's amazing we didn't all get wiped out because of this problem. We were lucky indeed that there were so few fatalities or injuries when we carpooled.

Carpooling in the fifties and sixties was done on a wing and a prayer. Many cars were patched and held together with baling wire. In the Lehighton area, several drivers started driving by themselves because they couldn't put up with some of the bad cars or bad drivers.

I guess I can thank my lucky stars that I got through all the years of carpooling with my body still in one piece.

SNOWSTORMS and FLOODS

ON SEVERAL OCCASIONS throughout the years, heavy snow put a damper on steelmaking. Workers on following shifts couldn't make it in to work when main highway arteries were closed because of high drifting snow.

In the plant, the rail lines and switches were buried under snow. Truck traffic in the plant was cut way back.

When huge snows fell there was no place for the workers to park their cars. It was truly a mess. The steel company made cleaning of snow from any of its parking lots a top priority in later years.

Joseph Elliott

Strikes weren't the only thing that brought the Bethlehem plant to its knees. Mother Nature also accomplished this. I know of two major floods (1942 and 1955). One was during my time.

In 1955 the water from the Lehigh River and surrounding areas cascaded into the plant, putting some sections under four to five feet of water and mud. The blast furnace and the surrounding shops took the brunt of the floods. Although I do remember that the water flooded out through the main gate almost to 3rd Street.

All the electric motors had to be pulled, dried, and cleaned. Once the water receded, the mud left behind was horrendous. Laborers were brought in from the other end of the plant for cleanup. Everyone got a lot of overtime. Some smaller heating furnaces had damage to the firebrick. Flues and chambers going to stacks had to cleaned and dried.

When the river flooded the plant, much of the water backed up through the storm sewers which exited right into the Lehigh River. The force of the water backflowed through these lines and lifted up the manhole covers and the water literally poured out into the plant.

Craig L. Bartholomew.

Construction of the flood wall, a U.S. Army Corps of Engineers project, along the Lehigh River in 1961.

In time, the city of Bethlehem and the steel company, through the assistance of the U.S. Government, put in a huge dike between the river and the railroads. In this dike is an enormous size pipe that helps hold back excess stormwater from the city or plant and then has a system to release it into the river without it backing up through the lines.

Once this dike or retaining wall was built, floods were a thing of the past.

SLOW TIMES — 1958 TO 1960

BETWEEN THE YEARS 1958 and 1960, a large amount of Bethlehem Steel's work force was either on layoff, or working a four-day week. Many of the work force were off for 18 months or more. Some were off for over five years.

At that time, if you were laid off for more than five years, you lost your job. In later years the union had this ruling changed and many of these people were reinstated. I personally heard of some workers coming back after being off from work for over eight years.

Anyone in the Lehigh Valley that graduated from the local high schools in those years found next to no work in the area. Lehigh Valley residents who were out of work had to go to New Jersey to look for temporary jobs. A couple of the fellows that had worked for the Steel and were laid off went to Greenland for work.

I myself took any job that came along, from emptying railroad box-cars of flour for the local bakery to filling in as a house mover. I also helped dig a couple of graves to make a few extra bucks. At that time, all these jobs paid a buck an hour. Any jobs that became available and you told them that you were laid off from the Steel, they automatically wouldn't hire you. They all said the same thing. As soon as the Steel calls you, you will quit and go back to them. How right they were.

I was offered a job with the state, working for PennDOT. When the superintendent of highways in my area asked if I would go back to the Steel if they called me, I had to say yes. I never lied and I wasn't going to lie. When I think about it now, maybe I should have given a little white lie. After all, how hard is it to say no? Telling the truth did lose me the opportunity of getting this job and I certainly needed it, but life went on!

Prophesying

One day when I was down at the Bethlehem Steel employment office, I stopped off at our carpenter office to talk with our clerk. He was very close to some of the bigger bosses and heard all the rumors about any potential work coming in. We had four or five guys in a car pool driving between 90 and 100 miles to collect five bucks a week.

He told me that I probably wouldn't ever be called back to the Steel. Just what I needed. He prophesied that according to the long-range plans, the hot end, especially the blast furnaces, was going to be shut down. He went on to say that the entire Lehigh plant from the New Street Bridge all the way up to the Army-Navy gate would be shut down and eventually demolished. At that time I thought that this had to be dumb talk, that this couldn't happen. Boy, how wrong I was!

Although it took 38 years for this prophesy to come to pass, it is now happening. In 1996 plans are being made for all the blast furnaces and many of the other buildings to be torn down.

A strange thing that happened is that when he mentioned about what buildings were going to be demolished, he didn't include the DE Annex buildings, west of the old New Street bridge. In late 1996 these buildings remain standing. They were sold or leased to other companies. It is ironic that this prophesy is coming true. In fact, right on the money. I do personally believe that this was all a master plan drawn up by the Bethlehem Steel Corporation to shut down most of the Bethlehem plant.

I think the reason the plant lasted as long as it did is because of the power of the workers union and the persistence of the union to try to keep the plant operating.

If you are not familiar with the Bethlehem Steel's plant location and did some studies about the site that the plant was built on, you would definitely wonder why it was built there in the first place. Actually the plant's construction started there because it was at the junction of the Lehigh Valley Railroad and the North Penn Railroad, and had access to the Lehigh River as a water source. The plant was originally built as a rolling mill to produce high-quality iron rails for the Lehigh Valley and other railroads. It was close to iron and limestone deposits, and anthracite for fuel was brought by train on the Lehigh Valley Railroad. When the company started making steel, the local iron ore did not work very well so they started to ship all the ore in from long distances. In the earlier years, starting in 1884, much of the iron ore came from Cuba, from the Myarri and Daiquiri mines.

The best of locations would be where there was access to ocean-going vessels to bring in the iron ore from the Great Lakes and South America. Shipping the ore to an unloading facility along the ocean or bays and then transferring it to railroad cars proved very costly down through the years. Direct hauling by railroad from the Great Lakes also was very expensive and when the ore froze in the railroad cars, this was an added expense.

The whole plant just "grew like Topsy." It certainly seemed like there never was any planning. If there was a space, they put in a building. Nothing was built with regard to other buildings. The roads in the plant certainly had no early planning. Some of the main roads ran between buildings and were only one lane wide and had hard 90-degree turns. In later years, some trucks had to go in reverse over long distances to get to loading docks. These roads were truckers' nightmares. The way the plant is laid out, there sure couldn't have been any thought to future expansion.

I have a section on pollution, but I would just like to tell how it was in my earlier years.

The No. 1 Open Hearth and the electric furnaces poured out smoke and dirt over the whole south side of Bethlehem. Whenever anyone traveled up 3rd Street or Emery Street, there were times you couldn't even see anything because of the dirt and smoke. It was truly bad. I remember putting on my headlights so other cars could see me. In time they placed a system that collected the dust, smoke and gases and ran them through a process that cleaned up this mess.

It is kind of ironic that most of the dust collectors and new systems of containing gas, dust and smoke that have been installed are all going to be shut down very shortly. The iron foundry, the steel foundry, and the ingot mold foundry all had good pollution controls in later years. In the fifties, there were virtually none. The ones that were in operation didn't do the job properly.

Bethlehem Steel paid out huge sums of money on all these pollution controls and it is all for naught. We have to remember that most of these expenses were written off their taxes, one way or other.

The shameful part is that Bethlehem residents put up with all the dirt and pollution all those years and now that the systems are working they are shutting down most of these facilities. Once again, we have to realize that when these shops or steelmaking operations of the plant are shut down, the Bethlehem Steel Corporation will get enormous write-offs. This will show up on the profit and loss columns, that's for sure.

In years past, some mills and operations that shut down were so antiquated that by shutting them down you did them a favor. The company took large write-offs for some of these facilities. Hell, some of these were shut down for years, and then when they were demolished they took a write-off. Strange indeed!

There is one foundry that should have gotten a large write-off and that was the steel foundry. The company spent huge amounts of money putting in different systems to help operate a better system and also to keep down the pollution.

This shop was operating at a 12 to 13 percent profit. In other words they held their heads above water. They did certain jobs that other foundries around the country couldn't do. They also used hot metal from both the electric furnaces and the blast furnace, which helped their economy.

What happened was that the prime rate of interest hit 20 percent. The chairman of the steel company at the time said that if any shop couldn't make over 15 percent profit they would be shut down. His reason was the Bethlehem plant could get 20 percent on their money. What I do remember is that at that time the company had a very poor cash flow and really didn't have any money to invest so it could get 20 percent on its investment.

Since the foundry could manage only a 12 to 13 percent profit they shut it down. I personally think that this was one of many mistakes that they made. But then again, this is what I heard as a worker. I didn't have access to inside information. In other words I only knew what they wanted me to know.

Layoffs

Through the years, I was laid off from my regular job at least ten times. Sometimes I was offered other work in different shops throughout the plant. These were all low-paying, mostly labor-type jobs. They kept the pay checks coming and I did have a chance to learn and observe different working conditions around the plant.

Some of the various departments that I worked for were Weldment, CSL Laborers, 405 Carpenters, 409 Riggers, 620 Billet Yard, ash man for Coke Works No. 5 Boiler House, Cinder Dump laborer, scarfer, Trucking Department (office), Ingot Mould carpenter.

The nice part of layoffs, if there is such a thing, is that I met and worked with many of my union brothers. Most were friendly and willing to show you the ropes. You did find a few workers hard to get along with, but, thank God, there was only a handful of them.

The biggest change I found when I took another job instead of an outright layoff was the time change in my work schedule. In the earlier years my department worked a day shift from 8 A.M. to 4 P.M. Most other departments worked their day shifts from 7 A.M. to 3 P.M. What this meant was that I had to find a new car pool or drive to work by myself.

The cinder dump, one of the many places where I worked. Drivers often stopped along Easton Road outside Hellertown to watch the beautiful glow of slag pots being emptied at night.

When I was in the labor gang, there were new workers coming and going every week. I must have worked with hundreds of different guys. Like I said earlier, some were different. One fellow from Easton had a piece of his ear shot off when fleeing Easton police. Some had very strange backgrounds. Some were just strange, like meeting one guy who was visited by aliens from another world. He swears to it! I also met some who were downright crooks. At home and at work.

The amazing part of the steel company is having thousands of workers, working together and having a lot of stress on certain jobs, and having very few fights or assaults on one another. Sure, there were disagreements on certain jobs. Some workers didn't like the way a lead person or foreman was running the show.

Our union had strict rules on fighting. If anyone punched someone for no apparent reason or otherwise, they were history. The union usually didn't even represent them. They ended up being fired. If there was a mild skirmish without too much personal injuries these cases were ironed out. Most of the time, when there was some large misunderstanding, there were threats and a lot of cussing. Usually that night most cooled down and everything was soon forgotten. I personally only remember one person who punched a foreman in the face. If I remember correctly, his job was terminated.

So all in all, the experiences of working with thousands of different people throughout the years in the Steel were not only interesting, but exciting.

Whenever I had a layoff, when I had no job and collected unemployment, this was like having an extended vacation. I took advantage of these layoffs and enjoyed them to the fullest. I fished, hunted, swam and had a ball, full-time. What else could a single guy in those earlier years ever want?

In the earlier years, salaries were low, cost of living was low, so unemployment checks of $40 a week didn't look too bad. Before my retirement I was earning around $16 an hour. Now when I think back on the $40 a week unemployment check, I wonder how I ever survived? Oh boy, I almost forgot, I did receive, each week, a five dollar supplemental unemployment check from the Steel. This was a program that was set up by the steel company. It seems that when it was my turn to get some of this easy money, the fund was almost depleted. In later years they had a guaranteed amount which helped anyone who got laid off. The unemployment check from the state along with a company supplemental unemployment check was nothing to sneeze at. It certainly made being laid off a little nicer.

ETHNICS

THE BETHLEHEM PLANT down through the years had mostly white workers. There were some blacks and Hispanics.

I never heard of any race problems and most of the different ethnic groups all worked together and got along. In fact, it wasn't until the civil rights people started telling the world that there was some kind of problem in the working place, that some blacks or Hispanics even gave it any thought about not being treated fairly.

To be honest with you, their education and abilities were just like mine: limited or average. We didn't have the training or a higher education to really get ahead as far as being a supervisor. This is only my opinion.

In the early fifties or sixties, most supervision in the Labor Construction Department of the Bethlehem Steel seemed to be either Windish or Pennsylvania Dutch (German). Whatever the supervision was, it seemed that they treated their own with better jobs, quicker promotions, and more overtime. I was certainly as white as they were but yet they looked more favorably upon their own.

There was nothing more annoying than when a foreman would talk to other workers in Windish or Pennsylvania Dutch. You always felt that they were saying something behind your back, and this is what was usually happening. Also in the early days, overtime was given out to whomever they liked best. Later, the union stepped in and most shops voted for overtime to be given to everyone. In other words, the overtime list was evened out in the end. Everyone got their fair share of overtime.

Well, sort of!

BLACKS

THROUGH MY 40 YEARS of work at the Bethlehem Steel, I have worked with blacks and Hispanics. There weren't all that many and it did seem like a token amount. There never were any race problems. We all worked together as union brothers. Sure some people were racist but they kept that to themselves. There was never any segregation, but this statement does have shades of gray.

When work was plentiful and the steel company needed laborers for the Coke Works, whites didn't want this type of work. They hired many Mexicans and then later Puerto Ricans to fill these labor jobs, especially the work on top of the Coke Works ovens.

The jobs on the ovens in the earlier years were horrendous. In time, some pollution controls were put in place and this helped a little. Real little! There was a saying at the Coke Works:

If you're sickly, the smoke and fumes would cure you.
If you're healthy, the smoke and fumes would kill you.

I always thought that the different races got along very well. One of my pleasant memories, and it is a memory I'll never forget, happened at the Coke Works.

In the early nineties, I was very fortunate to hit the Cash 5 Lotto that the state of Pennsylvania ran. I had many people come up to me and congratulate me. In the same case I had three close working buddies who said nothing.

While at the Coke Works, two black workers whom I had never met came up to me and asked if I was the guy who hit the Lotto. After I said yes, they shook my hand vigorously and congratulated me for my good fortune. They said they were glad to see a fellow steel worker and union brother hit the lotto. It did seem as if they couldn't congratulate me enough. I could honestly say, that these two fellows were happy for my good fortune.

These two gentlemen made me really feel good. It was a very proud moment in my life. This showed me there was no discrimination or jealousy over the race issue. We are all union brothers regardless of our color or ethnic background. I am very proud of this.

DRINKING and DRUGS

IN LATER YEARS, like the eighties or nineties, drinking and drugs did cause some problems. Some workers came to work drunk and caused some problems.

In the early years when you walked through the gate to get into the plant, there was a plant patrol standing there to check your badge with your department and symbol number. In later years, you walked past a machine, inserted your plastic identification card and a turntable opened up. If you were drunk out of your head, the machine didn't know this.

Drugs did cause some problems. It seemed that a few of the workers' brains were altered by drugs. The few who were on drugs full-time had some drug connections at work. They knew where to go at lunch time for "happy hour." Most handled it with limited problems, and didn't cause any accidents or problems. Some had an attitude problem because of the drugs. I personally didn't see too many that got drugged out of their minds.

The steel company handled drinking and drugs as an illness. Most who had problems got a good talking to. Some who missed work because of drinking or drugs got time off. But I only remember one person losing his job because he missed more than 10 days in a row without reporting off. He had plenty of warnings. The union helped him as much as it could. In the end, they had to get rid of him. When he wasn't on drugs or whatever, he did his work and was one of the guys. When he had his problem, he was difficult to work with. He had more than his fair share of warnings.

Ore trolley on the Hoover-Mason charging trestle. The ore was dumped into hoppers below, where it was weighed and put into skip cars. A steeply angled skip hoist can be seen behind the ore car. The trestle had three rails. Ore trolleys ran on a 9-foot track, and coke and other cars on standard-gauge tracks.

CASTERS

MAKING SLABS INSTEAD OF INGOTS

IT WAS IRONIC that a makeshift, experimental type of caster was built in the early sixties in the Lehigh section of the Bethlehem Steel Company. This was built in the Bethlehem plant before any of the other Bethlehem plants had one, or for that matter any steel company in the United States.

What I had heard was that several steel companies pooled their money or resources together to have the caster built at the Bethlehem plant. It was to be used for research or experimentation to see how it worked. I would also imagine this was to get any bugs out of the system or improve on it. The caster was patented by German companies. If this country's steel producers were to use it, they would have to pay royalties on every ton produced. I will assume that the American companies wanted to try the German caster and then improve or change it in such a way as to get their own patents, so that no royalties would have to be paid. This is my own personal assumption.

As far as casters went in the U.S. it was something new for the steel industries.

The purpose of this caster was to pour or cast the hot molten steel into slabs without using any ingot mould. A large expense in pouring ingots was the narrow-gauge railroad, which hauled all the moulds and ingots from the furnaces to the stripping facilities and then to the soaking pits. Casters would eliminate the stripping process of taking the ingot out of the mould. The moulds used for ingots had only so many hours of use before they cracked or developed other problems. The ingot moulds were quite expensive to build. Also, the slab from a caster would need fewer passes at the first blooming mill. So all in all, it saved time and money.

For the survival of any plant these days, it is imperative to have a caster installed, which would reduce the number of man-hours for every beam produced. Our union at the Bethlehem plant pushed for the installation of a caster. The corporation played around with this idea, but turned it down. If a caster had been installed, the Bethlehem plant would probably have shown a better profit margin. I don't think the top management people wanted this done. I still think that their goal was to shut the Bethlehem plant down.

Since late in 1995 they have been bringing blooms into the Bethlehem plant from Bethlehem Steel's Steelton plant to be used in the combination mill. The blooms have to be hauled about 90 miles. The cost of shipping these blooms to the Bethlehem plant will eventually bring this plant to its knees and give management reasons to shut it down. They have had to install a new type of crane to unload and load the blooms when they arrive from Steelton. Special trucks had to be ordered to haul them from the storage area to the pre-heating furnaces. These trucks have a price tag of over $600,000 each. They will need several of these trucks to keep up with production.

Rust Furnace at the combo mill. It is used to heat billets to rolling temperature. 1994.

Joseph Elliott

Keeping up with the Times

When they built the new combination mill and the basic oxygen furnaces, the corporation breathed life into the old plant. At that point it looked like the Bethlehem plant had a future. They were really a godsend. The two operations worked smoothly.

When the basic oxygen furnaces went on line, the old open hearths were abandoned. In time they were demolished. These old open hearths served the company well. The Saucon Number 2 and Number 4 open hearths between them had 19 furnaces. The new basic oxygen furnaces had two vessels which could be used together or alternately for steel making.

The open hearths took several hours to make a heat while the basic oxygen furnaces could make steel in 50 minutes. The old open hearth furnaces became a thing of the past. How ironic, that the basic oxygen furnaces put the open hearths out of business, and now the casters in other plants are putting the BOF out of business.

Which Plant Survives and Which Plant Dies

In the modern world of steel making it does seem to be a "dog eat dog" kind of survival. The plant that has the modern steelmaking facilities survives. The rest of the old antiquated plants go by the wayside.

There is one other pawn that determines which plant survives or which one dies. The people in top management seem to form some kind of bond to the plant where they were supervisors before going up the corporate ladder. They push for their plant to get the modernization.

Some states or cities give tax breaks for modernization of plants. Some also have lower corporation taxes. All these things seem to go into the pot to decide who survives and who doesn't survive.

New Combination Mill

Along with the construction of the basic oxygen furnaces, Bethlehem Steel installed two new Rust pre-heating furnaces and a combination mill that would make several different sizes of the smaller beams, angles and pilings.

The first steel rolled was a B8 x 20 lb. (20 lb per foot beam with an 8" web), rolled on 12/12/68. The combination mill equipment was designed to produce sixty 250-foot-long sections per hour. This mill was

Joseph Elliott

(Above) Cooling tables at the Combo Mill in 1994, where beams were set out to cool after being shaped by the mill.

(Below) Moving beams in the beam yards of the Combo Mill in 1994.

Joseph Elliott

54

much faster than the old mills they replaced. Also it handled more sizes than the older mills were capable of rolling.

These new mills were run with new electric motors. The older mills, except for one, were run with old-fashioned steam power.

Stand No.	Motor Horsepower
1	5,000
U2	6,000
E2	1,500
U3	5,000
E3	1,500
U4	2,000

The new mill was built mostly by outside contractors. I had the opportunity to do some work on it and I did other jobs nearby, which gave me the opportunity to watch its construction.

When they were constructing this mill, the supervision and engineers were claiming that this was going to be one of the newest type of mills around and that computers were going to be a large factor in its operation. The mill did prove itself up to their expectations as far as quality and speed were concerned.

One of the features that didn't come true was a clean operating mill. Boy, were they wrong on that account! They were claiming you would be able to eat off the floor. After a few short years, the building's floors and machinery were covered with oil, grease and dirt.

When the combination mill went on line, it was eventually responsible for the 28, 42 inch and the 12 and 18 inch mills to be shut down.

Mini Mills

The combination mill wasn't the only reason for the smaller beam and angle facilities to shut down. In time, mini mills started cropping up in the United States. They produced steel at a much lower price. This put a lot of strain on the different steelmaking plants. The Bethlehem plant just couldn't compete with the mini mills with price. It is very interesting how they could produce steel so cheaply. They did pay top wages to their blue collar workers, but expected their workers to give a good full day's work in return. One of the big savings was that they didn't have all the big management personnel running the plants. In the beginning, everyone was supposedly treated equally. That goes for workers and supervision. They didn't have any special parking privileges for supervision.

Their money was put into new modern equipment and not into fancy high-tower offices, expensive research buildings. More on this later.

Bethlehem Steel's quality of steel was much better than some of these mini mills, but some buyers of steel were only concerned with price. The modern technology of the Bethlehem combo mill made it much quicker and easier to change mills to make the different types and sizes of steel products.

The one market segment that the combo mill still holds and maintains is the rolling of steel piling in extra-long lengths. There aren't too many plants that can make and produce a piling like Bethlehem's combo mill.

The demand in the nineties for piling just isn't there. But in time it could be a godsend. As more beach fronts and shipping facilities are built along the bays or coast lines, piling will be needed. Even where huge mudslides are happening, where real estate prices are sky high, the piling may be the answer to future development and the prevention of major mudslides. Along the coast where beach erosion is getting bad, piling may eventually have to be installed to prevent further erosion.

Just a few years ago, the combo mills installed a system that checked and maintained real close tolerances of its products. This process gives the plant the leading edge when it comes to anyone needing or buying quality steel. There certainly is a big difference in quality between Bethlehem's products and some of the poorer quality of steel that comes off some of the mini mills.

ON TO THE RIGGER GANG

AFTER 23 YEARS in the 405 Carpenter Department, and feeling like a second-class citizen, I had the opportunity to bid out for a job with the 409 Rigger Department.

The biggest problem with the carpenter department was that they held their workers down. In the earlier years they wouldn't give certain people a chance to take tests. In later years the unions stepped in and pushed for allowing the workers to take tests every six months, if they so wished. Most of the young carpenters in years past got into the apprentice course. Others started as helpers and hopefully would go to "C" and then to "B" before they took their "A" test.

The "A" test was a series of eight or so tests that you had to pass. You had to make a combination storm and screen door in about 10 hours from scratch. That is, taking rough lumber and planing it down to the desired thickness. The tests were very unfair for field carpenters. Most of us field carpenters had never had a chance at using the sophisticated machinery in the carpenter shop. To make this door you had to use at least six different pieces of shop machinery. Most of us didn't even know where the on and off switches were for this machinery. I and a lot of other carpenters thought the whole setup for testing stank. If they wanted you as an "A" man you got it. If they didn't like you for some reason, you would never pass that test. They always found something wrong, no matter how small it was.

Most of the shop men had their own blades for the various machinery. What the field carpenter used was old, worn-down blades. This certainly didn't help matters.

When I got in the rigger gang, I felt like a first-class citizen from day one. The supervisors made me feel wanted. They encouraged me to take tests for a "B" rigger and then in six months for my "A" rating.

Many of the other riggers didn't open up their arms to greet us carpenters into their department. Many of these workers were apprentices. After four or five years some only had a "C" or "B" rating. Most didn't want the "A" because it did carry responsibilities with it. They didn't want it, but at the same time they didn't want you to have it either. I guess this is one of the down sides of human nature. I sure don't know what it is. Some of these guys failed to realize that we carpenters had paid

Joseph Elliott

Joseph Elliott

(Right) Sub car, out of commission, being repaired or prepared for relining with refractory brick. The worker on the right is one of the women in the plant.

Opposite (above) Slag or cinder pots and a submarine car being filled at "C" furnace. 1995. The slag pots carry slag to the cinder dump; the submarine cars take molten iron to the BOF or the ingot mold foundry.

Opposite (below) Closeup of a Treadwell sub car (made in Easton) being filled with iron.

Joseph Elliott

(Below) The trucks for a sub car were very heavy duty as they had to support the weight of both the car and its cargo of molten iron. The trunnions, which turned the car to empty it, were equally heavy duty. This is a Treadwell sub car. Behind it is a slag pot waiting to be filled.

Joseph Elliott

our dues. I had almost 28 years with the steel company at that time and most of those years it was with lower-paying jobs.

When I had six months in the riggers, my supervisors actually told me to put in for my "A" rating. With a little help from my burner and welder I passed the test. Qualified or not, I became an "A" rigger and damn well proud of it.

The rigger gang in time accepted me for what I was. Yes, a few begrudged me to the day I took my pension. One of the nice things about the rigger gang was that they all stuck together, and were a very well-versed gang as far as work goes.

There certainly was a lot of talent in the rigger gang. I know for a fact, that there wasn't any type of work or job that the riggers couldn't handle.

On many of the furnace rebuilds, a rigger by the name of Robert Kuzio, from Bethlehem, used to play the harmonica. During the Christmas season, he would play different Christmas carols. During other times of the year, he would play all the old-time favorites. Everyone enjoyed when he started playing his harmonica over the loudspeaker system. He always carried his harmonica in his lunch box.

The rigger welders were, without a doubt, the best all-around welders in the entire plant. I saw them weld patches on metal that looked like tissue paper. They welded in every position imaginable. These guys welded while wearing breathing apparatus in areas loaded with coke or blast gas. When the coke gas would become ignited the flames flared out of control, but the welders kept welding until the crack was sealed. These guys were good!

When some of the other departments had work that their own repairmen or maintenance people couldn't or wouldn't do, they got the riggers in to do the job. If the jobs were too heavy, too much climbing, too high, or too hot, dirty or dangerous, they called in the riggers. There was a certain respect for the rigger gang. When the chips were down, the riggers came through.

The many jobs we performed are too numerous to mention. I would just like to explain one job that the rigger gang had done.

Whenever a hot metal car (submarine) with a full load of molten iron would run off the railroad tracks and ground into the macadam and dirt, the riggers would be called to the rescue. At first the railroad would bring in extra engines and their own people with blocking, frogs and whatever to put under the wheels to get those back on the tracks. After several hours or so they would only make matters worse.

Then they called in the riggers.

Remember, just inside the walls of these hot metal cars was red-hot molten iron. There was always a threat of danger or death when working alongside or under these cars.

We would come to the job with 50 and 100 ton jacks, steel plates and steel blocking. Also many different sizes of hardwood blocking or timbers to raise the car or trucks from the ground. Some of the wheels on the trucks were buried halfway into the railroad bed.

We used large Pettibone-type cranes. On one occasion the hot metal car was jacked into the air and held in place with a crane while a bulldozer literally pushed the car onto the tracks. Yes, a little unorthodox, but we did get the job done before the load of iron solidified.

The riggers did a lot of climbing and rigging types of jobs. It was very fortunate that fatalities were held to a minimum and accidents weren't too critical. There were many close calls but the guardian angels of the riggers always seemed to be nearby. Stress at times was terrific. Stress probably took more of a toll than physical disabilities.

Riggers were known for their playtime or horseplay. Pulling jokes like pouring water on their buddies as they climbed ladders or as they walked under them, many a five gallon bucket of water got dumped on someone's head.

Of course if you dumped water and got caught or seen, you sure as hell expected your victim to get his revenge. Riggers were very vengeful and always got back, twofold. Sometimes it took a while, but you can bet the ranch it would be done!

I am proud to say that I never dumped any water on anybody or ever got any dumped on me. I don't think it was because I was that well liked, it was more likely that I was a little crabby, and a poor loser. I really didn't take to that kind of nonsense.

Another nasty habit was on a hot day, when a job was almost done, the water fire extinguishers would come into use. Most of this was done by the younger workers. It seems that they had to get the stress out of their systems and started squirting their buddies. Before you knew it, it was a full-blown battle. When the water extinguishers were emptied, many a water hose came into play. Thank God, no one ever got hurt or that a major fire never broke out with a pile of empty water extinguishers near by.

When working on high reach equipment, some of the young workers liked to extend the bucket all the way out and then go around in a circle, way up in the air. This scared the hell out of a lot of workers. It was dangerous and foolish, but this was fun to them.

Most of the shops that had shutdown weeks and had work done by riggers during the shutdown had a watchman to sort of keep an eye on things and on the riggers. Riggers had a bad reputation of, when the job was finished, cables, ladders and some tools would be missing. I don't know why. Hmmm.

The nice part of the rigger supervision was that they stuck with their men, no matter what. Even when we were guilty of some wrongdoings, our supervision spoke up and stuck with us. We were one.

I remember changing rails at the Number 2 Machine Shop's high run. This run was very narrow and dangerous. When doing work like this, there was a lot of stress. Some areas of the runs had a lot of grease buildup and it didn't help when walking on these runs or, for that matter, working on them. I myself had a few times that I slipped and sort of

Joseph Elliott

No. 2 Machine Shop, the largest machine shop in the world.

lunged forward, but caught myself in time. When this happened it scared you a little, that's for sure.

When we changed these rails on the high run, the machine shop had a watchman to work with us and watch for any fires. As we were burning off the clips from the rails, hot sparks or burning grease would fall to the floor. Around the various machines there were a lot of oily rags or cotton waste and these would catch fire occasionally.

Sometimes we would see smoke (no fire) coming from these rags. We would start yelling "Fire!" and the watchman for the machine shop would come running with a fire extinguisher. Before you knew it, every place we went to had smoke showing up. It seems that the people we had as ground men to hook up the new rails and unload the old rails had a little to do with the smoke.

They had this watchman going crazy. Somehow this took the stress off us guys working high up on the narrow crane runs. We did our job and it was done right.

Playtime is a must when dealing with stressful, dangerous work. Even our own supervision got into the act at times. A good laugh helped the guys get through that period of stress.

In parts of this book I mention about the stress in the work place, causing breakdowns and even suicide. Several workers in the Labor Construction Department committed suicide over the years. There were times that our department heads expected us to do the impossible, but riggers were known to do just that.

Cropped blank being rolled at the No. 1 stand of the Grey Mill.

48-INCH MILL OR GREY MILL
AND THE 59-INCH MILL

THE LARGEST OF ALL THE BEAMS produced by the Bethlehem Steel's plant came off the 48-inch mill.

These mills are two-high, driven by huge, twin-tandem reversing steam engines. The engines were loud and noisy but efficient as far as motors go. The story was that these big engines came out of old ships that were sent to the shipyards to be scrapped. This story was passed down through the years. I have found out that it is pure fiction.

These steam engines were tough as old work horses and just as dependable. They certainly did the job down through the years.

The largest ingots that the Bethlehem plant produced were taken out of the soaking pits and placed on a turntable, which would turn the ingot for the right approach for the first mill. This mill was called a blooming mill or bloomer. Then it went through a shear to cut each end of the bloom off. It then went to the 48-inch (the Grey mill) or later it was the 59-inch mill, which was called a shaping mill. From there it went through the finishing mill or No. 2 mill. Then one end was cut with a hot saw just before it went onto the hotbeds to cool.

The new 59-inch mill was run by a 10,000 horsepower electric motor. Although many of the 48-inch hotbeds, and foundations for some of the mills and most of the roller lines, were rebuilt through the years, the old mills and bloomers were the same old, original, antiquated machinery.

Being old didn't stop them from doing their jobs. This particular mill, the Grey mill, made production records throughout the years. These mills continually broke their own records. One good thing about the old mills was that they could be fixed and maintained by plant personnel. The repair or maintenance people kept them operating. The old saying of using baling wire and chewing gum came into effect here, many times. When the chips were down, the repair crew came through and usually in record time.

The new 59-inch mill was built in one area so the mill people could learn how to operate it and learn all there was to know about it. They also would work all the bugs out of the system. When it was ready for its permanent location, a special crane run was built to lift and move the

Joseph Elliott

(Above) Checking temperature in the soaking pits, where ingots are heated to over 2000°F. before being taken to the blooming mill, where the shaping process begins, then to the Grey or universal mill.

(Right) View down into a soaking pit as an ingot is being pulled out.

Bethlehem Steel Corporation

(Above) Looking west toward the shear and the roughing stand of the Grey Mill.
(Below) Shear of the Grey Mill. 1994.

Joseph Elliott

Joseph Elliott

(Above) Blooming stand of the Grey
Mill. 1994

(Right) Engine for the finishing stand
of the Grey Mill. 1994.

Grey Mill, second mill stand.

69

whole mill in one piece to its new foundation. It was an amazing feat. The moving was a coordinated effort by a lot of workers. It was done at a snail's pace and everything worked perfectly. It did take a lot of Yankee ingenuity to move it, but it was done without a flaw. Everything fell into place. My buddies and I spent over a year working on this project.

This new mill ran faster and worked like a charm. The new 59-inch mill is run with all the modern technologies known to man. Computers were a big part in its operation.

During the nineties, the demand for large beams started shrinking, so with the shutdown of the hot end in late November of '95, the old 48-inch mill rolled its last beam on October 18, 1995. What a shame. This mill made the steel company what it is today. To me, this has to be one of the major blunders of top management. I must be right in my assumptions because there are rumors at the time of this writing, that a mini mill is giving a lot of thought into going into large beams.

Joseph Elliott

Bethlehem's signature wide-flange beams in the beam yards east of the Grey Mill. 1994.

The mini mills take no chances. They must know something. They see a future in large-size beams. Could it be that the 59-inch mill at the Bethlehem plant would show too much profitability and be a determining factor in keeping the Bethlehem plant operating? Like I said earlier, I think that top management wanted to see the Bethlehem plant shut down totally. They seem to have been working toward those goals. Someone has been pushing for the Sparrows Point, Steelton or Burns Harbor plant to take over all the steelmaking facilities that the Bethlehem plant is now doing.

It is ironic that in the past, Japanese steelmakers were a constant headache to American steel companies with their cheap steel exports. Just recently some of my buddies at work have seen Japanese looking over the closed-down mill. Now, why in the world would the Japanese be looking at a mill that makes large-sized beams when this market is supposedly so depressed?

The 59-inch mill was fast, but the first mill or bloomer and the finishing mill were old and antiquated. If these two mills were modernized the Bethlehem plant's productivity would be hard to beat. A real money maker. It didn't make sense to change one mill and have a mill that feeds it, old and slow, and then have the last mill or finish mill also old and slow. These two old mills didn't help matter, that's for sure.

Closing of the 48-inch or Grey Mill

On October 18, 1995, the last beam was run through the old Grey mill or 48-inch mill. The Grey mill operated for 87 years. The 48-inch is among the oldest of the mills at the Bethlehem plant.

The name "Grey mill" came from Henry Grey, who invented it to produce wide-flange beams. When this mill was built around the beginning of this century, it represented a large risk for the company, because most steel companies questioned whether the new wide-flange beam would be any good. The scary part of this venture for the steel company was that Henry Grey had been turned down by U.S. Steel.

Charles Schwab, the president of Bethlehem Steel at that time, saw something good about this process and gave the go-ahead for the installation of a wide beam mill. This venture pushed the Bethlehem Company to be the number one producer of beams during the early years. It was because of the new wide-flange beams that the building of skyscrapers became possible.

How ironic that skyscrapers became popular through the invention of the wide-flange beam and now because of the decline of skyscrapers the 48-inch mill has shut down. There is no demand for larger beams. The 48-inch mill supplied steal beams and other steel products for the Empire State Building, the Waldorf Astoria Hotel, George Washington Bridge, Madison Square Garden, and on and on.

At the present time, the tallest building being built is only 30 stories tall. In the whole United States only 10 buildings over 20 stories tall are being built at this time. The problem is that most tall office buildings aren't fully occupied. Many are losing money.

In this time and age, tall buildings built on expensive real estate are no longer the norm. Suburbia is the way to go. Suburbs are much more popular because of better living areas for their workers. Land is so much cheaper. Because of this there certainly is no reason for expensive sky-scraper construction in this day and age.

TUBE STEEL

THE FOLLOWING IS what I saw and heard. Some of the information is an assumption on my part.

Here is an interesting story about how the number two steel company controls and sort of sets up a monopoly on a steel product that could have brought the steel company's regular mills, as we know them, to their knees.

In the early sixties, a new type of beam came on the market called tube steel. This was a new revolutionary type of beam, that could and would replace many of the wide beams that the steel mills produced. The steel tube was a four-sided beam. No flange. It was made in all types and sizes.

Its good points are that it was strong, easy to install and easy to work with. The best feature of all was that when it was installed, there was very little to do with it. It was a finished product. When you install a flange beam, you have to fasten wood nailers and then nail dry wall or paneling to cover the beam. When the tube steel is used as a column, there was no other work to do on it, except paint it. Also all the wiring, conduits, or other pipes could be run down through this tube.

The first time I saw this tube steel, some of my supervisors and engineering told me that tube steel was a threat to the very existence of the regular wide-flange beams. In a very short while after this, the company signed some type of agreement to handle all the sales on this tube steel. The Bethlehem plant became the distributor. I think that this was a big mistake by the producers of tube steel beams. The Bethlehem Steel Co. controlled their destiny.

Plant personnel cleaned out one of the buildings at East Lehigh and started storing the tube steel there. Our carpenter department 405 replaced the roof on this building. Our supervision decided on putting a new type of covered sheet iron on this roof. They made the mistake of ordering a lighter gauge of metal. What a mistake! When we were installing it and walked on the new covered sheet metal it bent under our weight. In time some of the screw holes stretched. The seams of the sheet iron weren't sealing properly.

The bottom line is that this newly installed roof leaked like a sieve. This certainly didn't help the tube steel that was stored there. It started rusting. Remember, when this tube steel was to be installed by contractors, all they wanted to do was paint it. Now they had to wire brush the rust off the tubes or prepare the steel in some manner for painting.

It is my personal assumption that the Steel Company never wanted this steel to get too popular, because it could have become the number-one preference over the wide-flange beams. In time, the tube steel just seemed to disappear from existence. I do honestly think that tube steel could have a future in the building trade, if the people who are in power give it a chance.

Joseph Elliott

Joseph Elliott

The huge blowing engines that delivered hot air to the furnaces were powered by blast furnace gas (CO). They were built between 1911 and 1930.

(Left) Blowing engine control room.

BLAST FURNACE DEPARTMENT

ALTHOUGH I HAVE NEVER worked for the Blast Furnace Department directly, indirectly I put in many hours with repairs and maintenance. On rebuilds, I was involved with every segment there was. I had the opportunity many times to be on the cast floor when hot molten iron flowed from the blast furnace into the hot metal cars. The process, although simple, was mind-boggling to the casual observer. The men who worked on the cast floor worked under a lot of stressful conditions. The heat, smoke and, yes, danger were there at all times.

The danger was there, but the men worked as a team. They watched over each other and of course they all knew their jobs well and worked with the greatest of professionalism. When the tapping of a furnace took place, one wrong move or step could mean death. They didn't work under fear, they worked always with safety in mind. Not only for themselves but also for their fellow workers.

The blast furnace's process would take an entire book to explain all its intricate details. I by all means do not know everything there is to know about this amazing process. I will explain just a few basics of the process of making iron, so that you readers will have a little understanding of what it is all about.

The heat above the molten iron is 3,000 degrees and they tap the furnaces about every three hours or so. They get approximately 300 to 500 tons of iron at each cast.

When the iron is ready to be tapped, they drill out the clay-plugged tap hole with an air drill to a point where there is a thin shell of chilled iron holding back the molten metal in the furnace. They then use a lancing bar to burn away this thin shell. When the molten metal comes out

Joseph Elliott

75

of the furnace there is a deafening roar from the pressure built up in the furnace. When the molten iron pours out, the smoke and dirt rise high above the cast floor. The red-hot molten metal flows by gravity through the vast array of runners or troughs of fire-clay and sand, until it eventually runs through pouring spouts into hot metal cars (submarine cars) placed beneath the cast floor.

Joseph Elliott

As dangerous as it looks there is something mystifying and foreboding about this whole process. The reds and yellows of the hot molten iron seem to dance on the surface as it races down the troughs. The hot molten metal seems to cast a hypnotic spell over those who stare and watch as this remarkable process is unfurled before them.

The above paragraphs describe what the casual observer sees. Now I will give a more detailed account of what is happening behind the scenes.

Joseph Elliott

(Left) Molten iron or slag flowing down a runner, with a mechanical dam raised, ready to drop down to divert iron and slag to different runners.

Before tapping the furnace, the materials for making the iron are hoisted up the skip in large cars, where they are dumped into the receiving hopper above the stack (the stack is the basic furnace itself). The height of blast furnaces, including the hearth, bosh and stack, varies. They can be up to 110 feet high. The stack contains alternate layers of ore and coke, together with limestones, findings, and sometimes sinter.

When the furnace is tapped the molten iron goes into a trough that flows into a dam, called the baker's dam, which forms a pool. The slag, which is lighter than the metal, floats to the top in back of the skimmer. The slag then flows through a side runner and through a spout into slag pots beneath the cast floor. When the cast is finished the tap hole is closed with an electric-driven piston, which forces about nine cubic feet of fire clay through a nozzle from a clay gun into the tap hole.

Joseph Elliott

Closing the tap hole with the mud gun.

Do I have memories of removing and putting the drill machine back into place! This drill is very heavy and is located in a hard-to-get-at location under a large bustle pipe. It took a lot of perseverance and Yankee ingenuity to do this job. Most of the time they would put in new anchor bolts. If my memory serves me right, there were 54 anchor bolts. The base of the machine had to be set just right before dropping it into place. It wasn't easy, that's for sure.

The blast furnace with its heat and molten iron looked like hell on earth. A controlled hell! It was a science.

Plans have been made to end the hot end of the plant, which will include the blast furnaces. The last furnace was banked in late '95. According to plans, these facilities will be put to the torch.

What made virtually millions of tons of iron throughout the years will now make scrap for some other furnaces in the corporation. All the wisdom that went into making iron from raw materials will be lost over time. The blast furnaces in the Lehigh Valley will be history.

On November 18, 1995, the No. 3 Blast Furnace (C Furnace) was cast for the last time at 10:15 A.M. The first iron was made in 1863 and the last in 1995.

As the hot molten steel flowed down the runways, one of the blast furnace workers whistled "Amazing Grace" over the loudspeakers. It was a sad moment for all the workers, as well as for the city of Bethlehem and the entire Lehigh Valley.

It took an hour and forty minutes to cast all the molten steel from the furnace for the last cast.

Having worked on several of the rebuilds of this furnace throughout the years, part of me is also gone.

Furnace crew at C Furnace, three nights before shutdown, Nov. 18, 1995. Ralph Attieh, James Briel, Ronald Meltzer.

POLLUTION AND CONTROLS

DURING THE FIRST PART of this century, up until the fifties, pollution was very bad. Pollution controls were minimal to say the least. At the blast furnaces, gas washers, dust collectors, and Dorr thickeners for removing the solids from the spent water were in place, but there were many old drainpipes emptying dirty, oily water directly into the Lehigh River. All the dust and dirt that was made during a cast went up through the roof monitors and vents.

When we worked on any of the roofs or high up on the charging floor of the blast furnaces we could see all the oil that formed on the surface of the Lehigh River. It was obvious to see where this pollution came from. There seemed to be a steady oil slick along the south shore of the river for a couple hundred yards along the banks of the river at the location of the blast furnaces.

It was quite interesting to see that during the early sixties for a short while the river did seem to be its cleanest.

From any high point in the plant you could see thousands of suckers and chubs flashing in the sunlight as they turned in the river while feeding. Even the surface had huge amounts of fish feeding off the surface. During the eighties you didn't notice this happening as much. Why, I don't know. Although whenever I went by some of the large drain pipes, you could see large carp feeding there.

In the early days the blast furnaces spouted every type of harsh toxic pollutant into the river for over 50 years. Mercury, arsenics, heavy metals were very prevalent throughout those early years.

Many storm sewers were located throughout the blast furnace area. I think that many of these were old lines which entered directly into the Lehigh. When we would get heavy rains all the dust and dirt pollutants would wash to the ground from the surrounding buildings or roofs and then flow directly into some of these storm sewers and eventually flow into the Lehigh River.

At the time I started this writing, plans were being made to shut down the hot end of the steelmaking plant. Now, in 1996, there are no more blast furnaces operating. The ongoing plans are to demolish these structures. I would imagine that from this point on, the Lehigh River will clean itself up and will become a great fishery once again.

(Above) The roofed structure between the furnace and the Lehigh is the cast house.
(Below) The sintering plant.

Up until the eighties, the cast floors of the blast furnaces had very little dust and dirt controls. This is where most of the dirt pollution emanated from. The Steel then installed huge hoods with a gigantic suction system that took most of the dirt and fumes and ran it through a modern system of dust collectors. Now, when all these pollution controls are in place, they are shutting them down.

In the sintering plant, the fine iron ore dust that blew all over the place would settle to the ground. When this was wet, it was just like greased lightning, as slippery as ice. Before the plant put in all the new modern dust-removal systems, most of the iron ore dust at the sintering plant would go skyward and be spread all over the place. When they installed the new roller line system and upgraded different pollution controls, then all the dust fell to the ground. There were piles one and two feet deep around the sintering plant. It was a constant battle for the sintering labor crew to keep up with this mess. It, too, has been shut down and is being torn down in 1996.

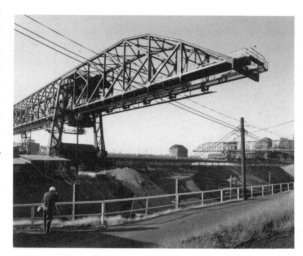

Ore bridge adjacent to the sintering plant.

Joseph Elliott

An interesting process that was built but only lasted a short time was a machine to solidify the hot slag as it poured out of the blast furnace. This was known as a pelletizer. The basic part of this operation was installed by outside contractors, but some of the 409 riggers got involved with certain parts of its construction.

Instead of the hot slag flowing into slag pots and then being transferred to the slag plant at the cinder dump by rail, the pelletizer would solidify and crumble it into smaller pieces that would fall to the ground. This way it was cooled down somewhat and it could be hauled in larger amounts, either by truck or railroad cars, to the slag plant.

What this process did was flow the hot molten slag through a sprayer-type setup. On paper this system looked like a winner, but when it went into operation the noise pollution was horrendous. Any workers on the cast floor couldn't hear anything over the popping sound of the slag as water hit the red-hot slag. The machine was nicknamed The Pop Corn Machine.

Normally when iron was tapped from the furnaces there was a very deafening roar as the hot metal flowed out of the furnace. The new popping noise over the top of the roar was too much for anyone to put up with. Workers at this point couldn't complain, because this system was supposed to be a godsend for the ironmaking facilities. Supposedly this system was going to make slag removal cheaper and in the end make extra money for the blast furnace department.

The steel company didn't realize that this noise would be one huge pain to the people who lived on the north side of the river. On the north side of the river was Moravian College, historical places, plus many doctors, lawyers and business people who didn't like the noise that came from this process.

Try as they may, the noise levels couldn't be reduced enough to satisfy these people. The Steel had to shut down this operation. Money and influence came into play. Big money won out. The Bethlehem Steel Corporation may have been a giant in the steel industry, but lost out to these people who lived on the north side of the river. It was a good process except for the noise.

Good Pollution Controls but not Enough

While I worked for the Steel, all the furnaces, different mills and foundries, including the new basic oxygen furnaces, installed modern, up-to-date pollution controls. They did operate efficiently to a point. But occasionally when there was a breakdown the skies would fill with big black clouds of dirt.

The Pennsylvania Department of Environmental Resources certainly didn't like this type of problem. Whenever this happened the DER would get large amounts of complaints over the telephone. I do know that when scheduled repairs were to be made on some of these systems, many of the times it would be done was during the night-time hours when the sky is black and the pollution wouldn't be noticed.

During the early years, the ingot mould foundry was a very bad polluter. During the seventies and eighties most of the dirt problems were taken care of. The ingot mould foundry has been shut down with the rest of the hot end. The ingot mould system was getting outdated. Most of the new steel was being made in casters, which don't need any moulds. It was just a matter of time when its usefulness in the steel industry would come to an end.

Throughout the Saucon part of the plant there were many different mills, preheating furnaces, soaking pits, hot and cold saws. These systems used a lot of water for cooling purposes. The engineering department came up with a new system to collect all the water, clean out the heavy particles of dirt, collect all the oils that floated on the surface of the water and then recycle it back through the plant. Instead of continually pumping millions of gallons of new water from the Lehigh, they would use the water over and over and only replace that water which was lost to evaporation. This was considered a closed system.

All the old water eventually ran to a deep pit located by the Saucon Pumping Station along the Lehigh River. This pit would clean out the heavy particles of scale, dirt, and grease. All the oils that floated on the surface would also be removed. The water was then supposed to be pumped into two large tanks that contained various-sized stones which would filter out the remaining solids in the water.

I had worked on this project off and on while it was being built. From day one, the field engineers had doubts about this system ever working properly. The first day they started the system they had major problems. No matter what they did, more problems developed. The stone filters in the tank got jammed with fine particles. Fine particles of steel also burned out the pumps.

If my mind remembers correctly, this system cost over 30 million dollars and never worked.

Reading between the lines, the only reason it was built was to appease DER and the Environmental Protection Agency. The Steel put off this project for so many years that the government agencies were going to place a big fine on the company. By starting the project. the steel got DER and EPA off of their backs. I sort of think the steel company didn't think it would really work but it had to come up with something. It turned out to be one gigantic waste of money.

Several years later, I had the opportunity to check out the pump house building and the tanks. The pump house was the heart of the system. Many of the motors had been taken out. It had been cannibalized. The large tanks sit there as monuments to a wonderful idea that went astray.

More Pollution Controls: Fewer Workers

As the Bethlehem plant got cleaner and less polluted, the workforce got smaller. Little by little, certain mills, foundries or shops shut their doors.

No one can say that the Bethlehem plant didn't do or try to do everything possible to reduce pollution. At the same time, many pollution controls were put in because of gigantic fines that were upcoming if the plant didn't reduce certain pollution problems. What seemed to happen is that DER or EPA would give the plant a period of time, sometimes several years, to come up with a certain plan and then to implement that plan.

The company may have been working on plans in the engineering offices, but it often seemed that the allotted time to have them installed came and went without anything being done. Then DER or EPA would set a new date, with huge fines to be applied for every day that the pollution systems were not in place. This usually was what was needed to get construction started. When DER or EPA saw for themselves that the work was being done in earnest, they would usually rescind or lower any fines.

There were times that the Steel paid out huge fines over pollution problems. This seemed to be the cheaper and easier way out. Some pollution construction costs were very expensive. While construction costs were high, operating some of these systems was also very expensive. As the systems aged, repair costs ran even higher. It took a lot of man-hours for repairs and maintenance on them.

The operations ran cleaner but the costs of reducing pollution didn't help the Steel's profitability. As paper losses mounted, this added more reasons for the management of the Bethlehem Steel Corporation to close some of the Bethlehem plant down. I really feel that the shutdown of the Bethlehem plant was imminent and was planned way back in the fifties, regardless of profit or losses at this plant.

WHITE COLLAR AND
BLUE COLLAR THIEVERY

THIEVERY AT THE BETHLEHEM plant is probably no different than anywhere else. Most workers had the attitude that the Number 2 steelmaker in the world could well afford it.

Up until 10 years ago, most of the vehicles that entered the gates at the Bethlehem plant were white-collar workers. Most blue collar or the regular workers had to park outside of the plant. Before the early eighties the gates were maintained by plant patrol. In the early years most workers had to open lunch boxes for inspections and at the end of the week most of the shopping bags that contained dirty work clothes got checked by plant security. At times they would put a hand on each side of the bag and press in while lifting the bag. If they felt something hard in your bag, or if the bag had too much weight, you had to empty it on the sidewalk in their presence.

Most of the petty thievery was small stuff, like nails, bolts, welding wire, pipe fittings. Something small to fit in one's pocket. Larger items went under overcoats or wrapped around one's body. More than one person wrapped rope, burning hoses, certain electric wire around their bodies and put on a large overcoat during the winter months. Most of the larger items that couldn't be carried past the plant security went out of the plant in supervisors' vehicles.

It was said that the workers stole retail, and supervision stole wholesale. Many workers felt justified in stealing small amounts of items in their pockets because they knew and saw their own supervision load up the big stuff in their vehicles. In fact, many of the workers were recruited into obtaining, preparing and loading of these very items.

Throughout the years, from day one when I started, I always heard that the Bethlehem plant wrote off over a million dollars for thievery on their profit and loss statements.

At this point some readers are probably wondering just how big that supervision or white-collar thievery really was? I saw a whole summer home of lumber, cut to certain lengths in the plant and hauled right out the gate. Even full-length beams were stolen right out the gate past security. This did take a little ingenuity, but believe me it was done.

Size didn't matter, there was always a way to get anything out of the plant. I remember when one of my buddies built a weight-lifting frame and none of the foremen at that time would haul it out for him. One dark rainy night, he hauled it out between the railroad and the river.

When supervision wanted to haul out something they always knew which gate was the safest as far as security went. Some plant patrol, or rent-a-cops in later years, were more lax. The old plant patrol also got their share of the loot. Believe me!

Most of the time, the security people didn't check out the cars that went out the gates. There was a lot of supervision who never took anything over the years. Occasionally, something large would be reported missing. Then every vehicle leaving the plant would be checked. They would check the trunks and under the seats of the vehicles. Whenever such checks happened, the word would get out all over the plant to watch yourself. Usually the items they were looking for were long gone, or were hidden till things cooled down.

While working in the carpenter department, I remember when several thousand board feet of white pine wood were missing. Another hot item was redwood. One supervisor had built a large redwood picket fence completely around his home.

There is no justification for stealing, but the blue-collar worker saw all this big stuff leave the plant and thought that taking a small bag of nails in his pocket out the gate was no big thing.

There were a few compulsive crooks among the ranks. One old-timer had a fetish of stealing paper towels. For years he would take one or two packs of paper towels every day. Nobody had the slightest idea what he did with them.

Please believe me, I am not casting stones. There were very few who never took anything.

I remember one time leaving our welfare room at quitting time. One of the hotshot plant patrol, who had a reputation of being tough on thievery, was walking by. He gave me a friendly wave and then his eyes dropped down to a paper bag that I was carrying. In this bag was a pound or two of ammonium sulfate fertilizer. He didn't say anything but I knew I was spotted. As soon as the plant patrol was out of sight, the bag got tossed over the bank. For the next few years the grass and weeds grew abundantly in that spot where the fertilizer spilled out.

This same plant patrol would go around inside the plant's parking lot and measure the distance from the ground up to the bumper. He would come back before quitting time and then remeasure, to see if there was a difference. I think this was for show. He wanted the plant's supervision to think that they were being watched.

Please don't get the idea that thievery ran rampant, because it didn't. Most people took a couple of little items whenever they needed them. Most supervisors didn't steal anything, but the few that did, did it big-time. One supervisor had a false bed in his pickup truck. This guy stole big-time. Even when the workers knew, nobody informed on them.

I guess there is a code amongst the workers.

(Above and left) Strikers during the 1941 strike, which resulted in the company's recognition of SWOC, the Steel Workers' Organizing Committee of the CIO.

(Left) The ERP was the Employee Representation Plan, a union sponsored by the company that had been created in 1919.

Courtesy, Ray Holland.

STRIKES

THE FIRST RECORDED STRIKE at the Bethlehem Steel Company was in 1910 and President Taft was president at that time. Taft was on the side of the strikers and had the Bureau of Labor investigate Bethlehem Steel's labor practices.

The president of Bethlehem Steel at that time was Charles Schwab, who called in the State Police and threatened to move the steel company out of South Bethlehem. At that point all the local business support of the workers dried up and the workers eventually went back to work at their old wages. The leaders of the strike lost their jobs. Schwab won his point: No worker would dictate company policy to him.

In those early years the workers had an organization called The Employee Representation Plan, that was run by the company and was created in 1919.

In 1939, the National Labor Relations Board told Bethlehem Steel that they should disband this organization because it was not a true workers' union, and didn't represent the working man, as it should.

In March of 1941 the union launched its first major strike since 1910. The State Police were once again called in, with their mounted police.

When I started working for Bethlehem Steel in 1952 many of these strikers told me all kinds of stories about what they did to "scabs" who crossed the picket lines to go to work. Some of the scabs' cars were overturned, others were vandalized, and some of the scabs got beat upon. A few had red paint dumped over their cars.

Being that the United States was on the verge of entering World War II, it was important that the company not go on strike. The pro-labor Roosevelt administration was not about to give out defense contracts to a steel company that had worker problems. So the steel company settled the strike by agreeing to recognize the Steel Workers Organizing Committee and collective bargaining.

The ironic feature of this strike's outcome was that a Bethlehem mounted police officer's horse rearing among the strikers became a classic symbol in labor, about police repression. This same man, Packard, was asked by the union to escort a victory parade.

In 1942, the United Steelworkers of America negotiated their first union contract with Bethlehem Steel.

In April 29, 1952, the union began a 53-day strike. Since the Korean war was going on, the government allowed the Steel to raise the price on a ton of steel to $5.65 a ton. This way union workers got raises and fringe benefits. On July 24, a settlement was reached, and 12 days later I started my illustrious career with Bethlehem Steel.

The next major strike was on July 14, 1959. This strike lasted 116 days. It was fortunate for me that I was laid off at this time and throughout the strike collected unemployment compensation. President Eisenhower issued an 80-day back-to-work injunction under the Taft-Hartley Law and the strike was officially settled on January 4, 1960.

My Personal Observations of Strikes

It did seem whenever we received something good or worthwhile, we had to give something up. It's also a fact that the Steel's main offices always had a running figure on what number of workers in the different wage categories had less or more seniority. In other words, they would give the most to the group with the least amount of workers. This group would receive more wages and also more benefits. The plant management did its homework quite well.

Down through the years, when the plant's contract was coming up, about a week or two before the deadline the plant would bring in hundreds of mattresses for the plant supervision to sleep on. They also brought in tons of extra food to feed everyone who stayed in the plant during the strike. I suppose this was to show the union that they meant business and weren't going to give in.

Strikes have definitely helped the common working man with better wages and benefits, but not without certain problems. Strikes also helped supervision get better wages and benefits also. When we got increases, supervision also got raises. Much more!

Whenever a strike seemed imminent, steel dealers, distributors and wholesalers stocked their inventory in case of a long strike. This did boost production for the mills. But if a strike didn't happen and there was a large glut of steel in the marketplace, this forced some shops and mills to have layoffs, or four-day weeks.

The biggest problem with pre-strike preparations was that many wholesalers or distributors couldn't get enough steel from the large United States steel companies so they started ordering steel from foreign markets. Many found foreign steel to be cheaper, even with large shipping costs. I personally saw a lot of this foreign steel and it was of very poor quality. Flanges were over- or undersize. The webs of the beams were thinner than American ones. There just didn't seem to be any quality check of this steel at their plants. Some flanges on the same piece of steel changed thickness and size in the overall piece. Some companies didn't look at quality, they looked at price. If they had to work with the scrap that the foreign mills were sending to our country they wouldn't have bought it. Problem was, that these buyers were basically distributors who sold to other companies.

After the strikes were over, many wholesalers and distributors started liking the idea of foreign steel. Their monetary returns were much greater and they in turn sold to retailers at a cheaper price. From this point on, the Bethlehem plant had to hold its price increases, while profits shrank. At the same time, buyers expected the quality to be top-shelf for Bethlehem Steel, but yet accepted the junk that foreign countries sold them.

In later years mini mills came into the picture. Most had no unions but they did pay good salaries and had good benefits for their workers. The mini mills had fewer white-collar workers and no country clubs, executive jets or airplanes, and no Taj Mahal-type offices. What they did do is put their investments into new mills and machinery. They expected their workers to give it their all and then some. Most workers in the mini mills liked working for these companies because everyone pitched in and everyone was treated fairly. Some had profit sharing, so if the company did well, you also got a piece of the action.

I must say with all honesty, that I worked with a lot of mini steel, such as angles and beams, and they were not quality steel. Even when the burners or welders worked with this steel, they had problems. The quality of the makeup of the steel was poor.

Once again I must be fair. Perhaps this was a bad batch of steel that was destined for the scrap heap and some distributor bought it and resold it to other companies? The distributor might have sold it, as is. I do know that the Bethlehem plant got some of this steel when certain building projects were given out to outside fabricators.

Whenever the Bethlehem plant had bad steel come through the mills, if it was beyond repairing it was scrapped and remelted into new steel. The mills did fix minor blemishes. They would chip out the bad section, weld it and then grind it smooth. The workers on these repairs put in many hours of overtime and were considered to be among the highest-paid workers in the plant. The rollers, the men who operate the controls in the pulpit overlooking the roller line, in some of the mills were one of the highest-paid work classes in the steel company.

In the eighties, givebacks seem to have become popular. The workers in the steel companies sacrificed and followed suit of what was going on around the country. The union and the Steel tried to work together for survival. In the end the powers that be, who wanted to shut down the Bethlehem plant, seemed to have their way. Not an instant shut down, only a slow death.

SAFETY AND WELFARE

INJURIES AND DEATH

THROUGH THE YEARS I have sat in numerous safety meetings where our supervisors explained how and why certain accidents had happened. One thing about the steel company, it always made it appear that it was the worker's fault. All reports stated: "Man claims..."

To be fair to the steel company, I want everyone to realize that the company had a very good safety program. They stressed safety at all times. Safety equipment was always available. If it wasn't there they soon got it for you. Many shops had a safety supervisor to implement different safety programs.

Safety posters were posted on bulletin boards all over the plant. Dangerous conditions or areas were well marked, but regardless of the amount of preaching and insistence on certain safety procedure, workers still had accidents, with an occasional fatality. Through the years I saw or heard of many deaths in the steel company. Regardless of the accidents or fatalities, it is safer working in the steel plant than involvement in certain sports outside of the company.

The deaths were varied. Death from breathing gases, falling from crane runs, being burned to death with hot metal or slag. Several workers died from a wall of a soaking pit falling on them. Some were caught between machinery in pinch points and died. The steel company had several deaths caused by electrocution. One electrician fell from a cherry-picker basket as he attempted to get out of it. One worker died from extensive steam injuries.

Working in the beam yards the threat of having legs, hands or fingers crushed or removed was always prevalent. The beam yards had safety hooks or rods handy all over the yards, so no one had to place their hands or feet in a dangerous area. As human nature will have it, the hands were still used off and on. Sometimes with bad consequences.

Everyone in the plant is issued safety glasses. If they get pitted, scratched, or broken they are replaced free, with no questions asked. I hated and fought against wearing these glasses, for over 25 years. Finally I had to get prescription glasses and from that time on wore them faithfully.

Thinking back, some of my supervisors preached, hollered, and threatened me with time off unless I would start wearing my glasses. I did wear them when I thought there was some danger from flying particles or when conditions warranted. Remember, these safety glasses were good quality, but they were also one-size-fits-all.

When you go for prescription glasses, they measure the bridge of your nose and work on the two arms that go around your ears. They heat them and bend them until they are comfortable. Probably the one-size-fits-all weren't really the right size for me. Even the arms going along my face to my ears pressed in on blood vessels, nerves or whatever and gave me a headache at times. I would bend the arms, bow them, and try to make them fit but I still hated them with a passion.

At one point when I was in the carpenter department, one of the field foreman said that if he caught me one more time without them he was going to send me home. He came back and there I was without the glasses. He sent me back to the office for discipline. When I got there my foreman asked, "What's the problem?" I told him the damn glasses were giving me a headache. He sent me to the plant dispensary, where they gave me two aspirin and told me to lie down on one of their beds. I had a nice hour-long nap. This type of punishment I can handle.

The nurse had compassion for me. She probably hated wearing glasses also. She did admit that they were a pain, but said to please give them a chance and wear them, that it was for my own good. Good advice, but it didn't make them feel any better.

Safety glasses, helmets and shoes on the night crew at the Electric Furnace Shop. 1992.
From left: Ed Zelina, 3rd helper; Ray McFadden, charging machine operator; Ernie Bohar, 1st helper; John Fielding, metallurgist; Cliff Meckes, 2nd helper. Zelina, Bohar and Meckes are equipped also with blue cobalt or melters' glasses.

As I wrote earlier, the steel plant had a lot of potential for getting yourself injured. During my employment with Bethlehem Steel, they had at one time four dispensaries. The following is an excerpt from a bulletin that I had read:

MEDICAL DIVISION:

The Medical Division is responsible for the operation of a Medical Center, a medical employment unit, and four out-lying dispensaries. The staff of doctors, nurses, technicians, and attendants render the following services: complete treatment for injuries and occupational disease; emergency treatment of personal illnesses; a complete hearing conservation program; examination of all employees returning after absence from work for any cause; pre-employment and pre-placement examinations, including a complete medical record of all employees. The medical division also works with the Compensation and Social Insurance Department on all claims. They give periodic examinations with special emphasis on supervisory applicants for gas school training and all employees who have been found to have physical impairments such as heart or lung diseases, etc. All personnel exposed to occupational diseases are given regular periodic examinations including chest x-ray, blood counts, and other laboratory tests required for diagnosis.

They had a complete modern clinical laboratory at the main dispensary. Whenever a bad accident happened they had an ambulance and crew right on the scene. It was always a comforting thought that these facilities were available to us. At times they had three or four full-time doctors on staff, and over a dozen or more nurses on the payroll. They had X-ray technicians, ambulance drivers, etc.

This gives you an idea of how many injuries happened every day to the workers in the plant. Many of these were minor, such as splinters, steel slivers. Dirt in the eyes was something that happened quite often.

The Steel took care of its workers. The management did everything in its power to prevent accidents but when they happened they gave you excellent treatment. When the dispensary couldn't handle the problem they sent you out of the plant to see a specialist. They even asked if you had any preferences as to what doctor you would like to go to.

One particular accident happened when I was working for the carpenter department. We were replacing a sheet-iron roof on one of the buildings in the sintering plant. We needed some type of chicken ladder to work off when replacing the sheet iron. One of the guys found one to use but it had no rope to tie it fast. I walked back to the carpenter shop for some rope but found out there was none available. One of the other guys in our gang found an old rope in one of the other buildings. The rope looked a little frayed but it seemed OK. We should have used brand-new, never-used rope. At times our carpenter department got reams of new rope, but we did use them until they literally wore out.

As luck would have it, me and another buddy were working on the ladder all day Friday. It was on the southeast side of the roof. If the rope had broken then, we would have dropped about 75 feet to machinery below. We both would have been history, that's for sure.

That weekend we had off and the following Monday morning two other buddies used the ladder on the southeast side of that particular roof. About two hours into the shift, the rope broke, and both buddies fell about 15 feet to another roof and then slid down into a steel walkway. Both men had back injuries and were hurting bad. One of the workers that got hurt also hurt his leg. This problem with pain in his leg persisted until he went on pension. The dispensary and outside doctors worked on this problem for a couple of years. One doctor made the comment that it was all in his head. We, his friends, knew different. The pain was for real.

From this point on, all ropes used on any ladders had to be brand new when starting any job. When the job was finished, the rope was supposed to be discarded. In all fairness, there was no one at fault but ourselves. We all saw this rope. We all knew that it was old. We took a chance and lost. Thank God, no one got killed.

The bottom line is that in a huge steel industry, danger is always lurking nearby. The minute someone got a little careless or indifferent an injury or death was imminent.

Stress was always there on our jobs. In the carpenters or the rigger gang we had all types of dangerous conditions to work under. We all took chances. A lot of stress was also carried into work from happenings outside of the steel plant. In work it was compounded with some of our jobs. Some also had problems with drinking or drugs.

I am sorry to have to write, but a few workers that I knew and worked with, including one boss that everyone liked, committed suicide. The stress was there, no question about it. I do think that certain medicines or drugs that several of these guys took helped push them over the line.

The Medical Center

The Medical Center and dispensaries were at their largest probably into the late seventies, but as the Bethlehem plant started shutting down certain shops or operations, they also reduced the number of employees.

The Medical Center did a fine job on minor injuries and on first-aid cases. Most of the injuries they treated were of smaller nature, although when serious accidents happened the plant personnel were the first to administer any first aid or help, before the patient was taken to a local hospital.

The Bethlehem Steel plant had a policy that they wanted you to go to the dispensary, no matter how small the injury. Many of the injuries were minor: wood or steel splinters, injured fingers, hands or feet, and a lot of cases of dirt in the eye. Burns were also treated at the local dispensaries. The nurses would clean the wound, and put on new dressings almost to the point of where the wound would almost be gone. We all thought of this as a little overkill. The truth of the matter is that they were concerned more about infection setting in.

Lehigh plant dispensary.

At times, many workers would treat their own minor injuries and then have them get infected down the line. Then the worker would ask for a dispensary slip. At this point, hell would fly. Some workers would even be threatened with time off (without pay) because of this. If a bad infection set in, the worker could lose some work time, which would then be considered a lost-time accident and the injured would be put on workman's compensation. In the earlier years, this was a big no-no. They didn't do this unless absolutely necessary.

I myself didn't report an injury one time. I was working up at the ingot mould foundry as a 405 carpenter. We were taking down a scaffold, when I jumped about three or four feet to the ground, something I did countless times. This time there was a nasty pain. After an hour or so, I shook the pain off and worked the rest of the shift without any problems. When quitting time came, we had to walk back to our carpenter shop which was over a half-mile distant. I started limping and my buddies asked what was the matter. I told them my foot hurt like hell, and I didn't know why.

That evening at home it did hurt, but with a little rest it felt good in the morning. About a week later the pain started up again and I asked for a dispensary slip. I told the dispensary people that I thought I had hurt it about a week or two before. This was the wrong thing for me to say. Then they fired the questions at me; Why didn't you come in? Why didn't you get treatment? At this point I had no answers, but as I think about it, I really couldn't go into the dispensary at quitting time, because I drove in a car pool, and these guys would have had to wait an hour or more for me to be treated. The next day, it felt better. How could you treat something that didn't hurt?

Anyway, the bottom line is that they brought me before a medical review board which claimed that I didn't hurt this foot at work. To me, this was one of the most stupid of deductions I had ever heard. When I went back to my department, my foreman said I was lucky that they came up with that verdict, because he would have had to give me a day off for not going to the dispensary.

In all honesty, my foot did get hurt when I jumped off of that scaffold.

By 1992, there were large buy-offs to reduce employees. By this time all the smaller dispensaries were shut down and only the main dispensary in Lehigh was open. The staff was cut way back. Two doctors were on hand and only a couple of nurses were on day shift. Middle and night shifts I think only had one nurse on duty.

During the nineties, whenever an employee had any kind of accident or injury, and if the dispensary wasn't helping him or her after a short period of time, the patient could ask to see an outside specialist.

It also seemed from the mid-eighties until I retired more workers were put on workman's comp than ever before. In the old days, as I wrote earlier, the company did everything possible to keep workers off workman's compensation. Some shops took pride that no one went on workman's comp or even had no lost-time accidents in years.

In the earlier years, shops would take care of anyone who became injured to a point where they couldn't do their job. They would place him on light duty. Some of this was assistant tool room man, watchman, cleaning up the shop or office, or just sitting in the office or welfare room doing nothing. You also received your full wages at this time. Later, they tried to reduce your pay to labor.

The injured were carried by the shops or departments to cover up lost-time accidents. It worked as far as keeping an accident-free record going. At times this did go a little too far. The plant patrol would take a plant vehicle to the injured person's home and bring him into work. Sometimes these guys had a cast on some part of their body, or walked with crutches or canes. They just sat around all day.

Doctors were also responsible for keeping workers off workman's compensation, even when they knew that a person was in serious pain and needed an operation to correct it.

Case in point: I had torn both my knee cartilages in a work-related injury. When I tore the first knee, I heard a loud popping sound and then felt severe pain. In later years I had this happen two more times and found out that when there is a popping sound from the knee, with severe pain, it is a torn cartilage. This is a text-book fact.

When I tore it originally, the doctor knew then and there that this was the problem. The doctor would also give it a certain type of twist which would induce pain and this showed him that it really was a torn cartilage. The doctor never told me this was probably a torn cartilage. They x-rayed it, which doesn't show tears in the cartilage, then he said it was probably just a sprain.

They would ice it, heat it and give therapy, three times a week. Over the weekend I would ice it, elevate it and give it plenty of rest. The knee felt great Monday morning. By Monday afternoon it hurt like hell, once again. This went on for over eight weeks when I finally told him I had had enough of this pain and nonsense and wanted something done. The doctor said, "I don't know how you put up with it this long."

A funny incident happened when I was working at a blast furnace rebuild and my knee was really sore. At quitting time I was limping real bad. When we headed back to our shop, we had to cross the main road going through the plant. The first driver in the lane of traffic waved me on. On his face he had a real peculiar look. When I looked back, about twenty other riggers were behind me in single file, all limping in unison to my limp. I had to laugh so much, that tears ran down my face. I don't know if I laughed at the riggers or the bewildered look of the driver waiting for us to cross.

In those earlier days they were reluctant to send you to an outside specialist, because they knew the outside doctor would operate and then there would be a lost-time accident. Years ago, knee operations would take about six months of recovery. In later years, with micro surgery, you could be back to work in from two to eight weeks, depending on what kind of work you did. Like I said earlier, mine was a text-book problem and the doctor knew that my knee had torn cartilage just from my explanation of hearing that popping sound. But they just would not admit it.

When I tore the rotator cuffs in my shoulder, they said it could be a sprain, tendinitis, bursitis or just "getting old" pains. Never did anyone say that it could possibly be torn rotator cuffs in my shoulder. When I went to therapy, a young therapist put me through the tests of pulling, twisting and what have you. She soon saw that I had excruciating pain when the arm and shoulder were maneuvered in a certain position. She whispered to me that it looked like this was a tear in the roto cuff area. She was correct in her diagnosis of my injury.

The company sent me out to their specialist and he gave me a couple of shots of cortisone in the shoulder, which didn't help whatsoever. He then sent me to St. Lukes for a dye and x-ray test on my shoulder. This showed nothing.

The pain persisted, so I asked to go to a specialist who I heard was sort of an expert in such matters. Right off the bat, he said "You have a roto cuff tear in each shoulder." I asked, how come the dye test didn't show this problem. He explained that the tear is on the bottom of the rotator cuffs and wouldn't show up with their tests. Why didn't the company's specialist know this? I guess this is something he just didn't want to admit. I guess the company doctors just wanted the pain to go away naturally.

The steel company got more than their share of knee, shoulder and back injuries. Outside therapists came into the plant on Mondays, Wednesdays and Fridays. On any given day all the beds or work tables were filled. For a couple of hours each day they had a steady stream of patients coming in for therapy. The therapy would help, but after it was done most of us would go back to our departments and put in a full day of work at our regular job. This aggravated the injury. It just seemed to be an unending battle. Therapy and then pain.

The bottom line here is that the steel company doctors had to answer to management if there were too many lost-time accidents. Also the shops or departments could take care of only so many "Light duty work cases" working at any given time. The doctors did their best.

Not every worker was totally honest, especially when it came to bad back problems. Some workers who hurt their backs took advantage of their problems to get on SIP or workman's compensation.

I personally know that when you hurt or pull your back it can be very painful one day and then could feel like a million dollars the next day. When anyone with a bad back feels good, they will lift heavy objects without thinking twice about the consequences.

Most doctors have a very hard time diagnosing a sore back. Some workers became expert actors when it came to faking a bad back. Most workers who hurt their backs were honest with the company about their problems but there were always one or two bad apples who spoiled it for the rest of the guys who had bad backs.

Our steel union never wanted anyone to lie or pretend about having any back problems, but at the same time tried to convey the message to the guys who had bad backs to do no lifting, regardless if the back felt good at the time. They always recommended that we should get some help to lift heavy objects and never lift them alone.

The union told us various ways that management used to catch workers who were on SIP or workman's compensation doing lifting. In most cases the workers would be videotaped doing the lifting. One trick that management supposedly used was to deflate a tire of someone's car and then videotape that person taking off the deflated tire, and then reaching in the trunk to remove the spare tire and mounting the spare onto the car.

Another trick was to call the person with a bad back and tell him that he had won a case of beer. They then supposedly videotaped that person picking up the case of beer, and bending over and placing it in the trunk of his car. Another worker was filmed picking up large stones and doing all types of yard work around his home.

Once again, workers with legitimate bad backs do have good days and when the back feels good, most don't give a second thought about picking up a heavy object. So this type of test was not always conclusive to someone being dishonest about having a bad back.

(Above) Canon barrel for a 16-inch gun outside No. 8 Machine Shop.

(Left) Quenching a 440,000 lb. generator forging at No. 5 High House.

(Opposite) No. 2 Machine shop with gun barrels and various other military contract items on the floor.

GUN BARRELS, SHELLS,
AND NUCLEAR HARDWARE

DURING THE FIRST WORLD WAR, the Bethlehem Steel Company at the Bethlehem plant was the largest munitions plant in the world. Also during the Second World War many shells and armaments were produced by this company.

What a lot of people don't realize is that this plant forged and machined many of the larger-size gun barrels for our government, all through the years, even during peacetime. Gun barrels were forged, then heat treated and sent to the machine shops for boring and rough finishing. Some of these gun barrels were shipped to other plants for the final machining; at least this is what I was told.

The Bethlehem plant had all the facilities to do this type of work. They had deep vertical furnaces for heat treatment. They also had large tanks for oil or water annealing. The Bethlehem plant has two high-

Bethlehem Steel Corporation

houses with deep vertical furnaces that can be used for the longest gun barrels or shafts.

I think it was during the late sixties or seventies that the plant installed a new rotary type of furnace at the Number 3 forge and treatment, for making large shells to be fired from the navy's larger ships. Three forge made the large 16-inch gun barrels and also the 175mm. The shells the forge was producing at that time were for the 16-inch gun barrels.

The plant spent a ton of money building this furnace. It was only in operation a short time, when the government stopped ordering these shells. Now it sits idle. They did use it for heating some other type of forgings off and on.

The government gave the Bethlehem plant large contracts for certain nuclear hardware. Some of these were for nuclear motors on ships. There also were some thick-walled steel containers for burying nuclear wastes. These were supposed to last at least 500 years.

I do know that laying out the material for the nuclear motors was really very intricate because of the different angles or pitches that had to be machined on them.

One of the inspectors of these products carpooled with me.

As nuclear-powered ships got more popular with the U.S. Navy, the Bethlehem plant received a lot of work, with some nice lucrative contracts. At the time it was a godsend for the No. 2 and No. 8 machine shops. It did keep them in work. This work also helped the hot end and the forges. It lasted for a few years until the cold war ended, when orders for this material also ended.

At the No. 1 Machine Shop, or the old No. 8, they are now making smaller nuclear devices for submarines. They are also making the 22-inch shafts for ships. These shafts are 60 feet long. Hopefully, some of this work is starting to pick up, once again.

OUTSIDE CONTRACTORS

THE BIGGEST PROBLEM when I worked for the Labor and Construction Department was that we knew that the corporation wanted to get rid of this department. We all knew that they wanted to have outside contractors come in and do the job, and then leave. Our union local was just a little too powerful for them to have their way. But now in the nineties, I think that the union is losing ground. Management is now getting their way. It was either go along with management's plans or have the whole company close down. These were not idle threats. I do think that this will happen down the line.

With the outside contractors, most of the work was on a cost-plus contract. At times, some of the work was put out on bid. The nice part of outside contractors as far as the company was concerned, was that they didn't have to pay vacations, health and life insurance, social security or unemployment taxes on these workers. They didn't have to worry about them getting sick or going on pension. The company liked the idea of getting the outsiders in the plant when they needed them, and then have them leave when the job was done.

In the earlier years, iron workers or boiler makers did a good job when working for the steel company. In later years it was my observation that they didn't quite do the best of work and at times the work wasn't done properly. For some reason, when the work wasn't done properly by the outsiders, our plant workers would have to go over it and do it right. Our office used other charges and covered it up. To me, this looked like a little hanky panky. A genuine cover up!

Hiring outside help to supplement the work force when needed was fine. But at times it seemed that management flooded the steel with all kinds of contractors to get the work done, and then laid off their own workers because of a lack of jobs. This type of happening was quite prevalent when I worked for the carpenter department. I personally think that the head of the Labor and Construction Department was responsible for this unfair treatment of its workers.

One thing was for certain, they never laid off their own white-collar workers. The Labor and Construction Department had superintendents, assistant supers, and a lot of other excess baggage. They had their own offices and a lot of other goodies. The workers had to carry these people.

Many of these so-called supervisors didn't carry their own weight. They were nothing more than figure heads. Whenever our department had to figure a cost for certain jobs, the price per man-hour was extra high because of us workers having to carry all this extra office personnel.

All the small departments that made up the Labor and Construction Department also had general foremen, assistant general foremen, shop foremen, field foremen and clerks. One thing the steel company had plenty of was office people. Most did a good job and got things done but some were just one big waste of money.

I think the ratio of workers to bosses was something like one to seven. Even in prisons the ratio of guards to prisoners isn't this close. This is one of the reasons the outside contractor can do a job cheaper than plant workers. They don't have to carry all the dead weight.

Since the early '90s outside contractors have been tearing down sections of the plant. Left to right, the powerhouse, furnaces, trestle and partially dismantled No. 3 High House. 1992.

SLEEPING ON THE JOB

AT THE TIME THAT I was writing my memoirs, I was at a barber shop getting my hair cut. I was talking about the Steel when the barber asked me a question that I have heard countless times before. He said, "Does everybody at the Steel sleep all night when they are on midnight shift?" He also asked, "Does the foreman wake you up when he needs something done?"

Oh boy, is this a misconception! Most workers on midnight shift didn't sleep most of the night. Yes, in some shops or mills some repairmen did get away with this at times, not always. Most shops or mills had token numbers of repairmen out. After a little regular maintenance work they got a long break and some probably slept most of the shift. But if there was a breakdown or something else came up, then sleeping was out.

In many mills or shops, anyone that was an oiler, greaser, or motor inspector usually had some good breaks. There were a lot of good jobs in the steel, but on the other hand, there were more lousy jobs than good jobs.

I do remember saying this quite often. I would tell the guy with the soft job, that if I could ever get another job, I wanted his job. Some guys had some sweet positions.

I wrote in another section of this book, when I was scarfing for the 620 Billet Department in the early sixties we got a 10-minute break for lunch, and that was it. Whether you ate or slept for 10 minutes, that was up to you.

In the laborers, when we worked hot work in the mid-fifties, we had three gangs spelling each other. You definitely lay down between spells, especially on midnight shift. When we did open hearth work, there would be dozens of planks and boards all over the place, used as beds. In the morning they would be all gathered up, so supervision wouldn't get bent out of place. But they definitely knew what was going on.

In the winter, you looked for a nice warm place to lie down. In the summer you went outside, under the stars, to cool off.

Let me clear up this sleeping business. When you worked in a real hot area, you would come out of the job site soaked to the skin with sweat. Your mouth was so dry you couldn't even spit, no less swallow. You had cotton balls in your mouth. The first thing you did was head to the drinking fountains. The wise worker rinsed out his mouth a couple of times and sipped on the water. Believe me, you wanted to gulp down the water but you learned better. Most of the new workers took big slugs of water, became bloated and then got sick as a dog. Many had to go to the dispensary. Even when I took smaller mouthfuls of water, I had a sick-like feeling. So lying on the planks wasn't always pleasant times. While you lay there you just wished the night was over and you could get the hell out of there.

I also remember working down in the beam yards on some major construction. The laborers would give you a half-hour break on the midnight shift. Many of the workers were so tired or sleepy that when they went to the toilet, they fell asleep. When they came back 20 minutes later, the labor leader wanted to know what took them so long. Most just said that when they went next time, they would bring back a sample. That usually shut up the leader, because I think he thought they meant it.

When I was in the carpenters, and if we had a big job going on, they gave you a half-hour break. Sometimes a little longer. If we were out servicing another craft, you could read books or magazines (this was not tolerated on day shift). Some lay down until someone needed your services. Some nights you did nothing, but this only happened occasionally. There were times as a rigger or carpenter that we were scheduled out to start a job on a press or furnace and it never went down. You did have a good night.

It does seem that in the earlier years, getting good breaks wasn't as prevalent as in more recent times. In the old days, the foreman would go look for something for you to do, even if the work was meaningless.

When I was in the riggers, we would work right through our coffee break and really dig in so we could get a longer break. Supervision was happy with the work accomplished, and we also had a decent night.

I remember putting in wooden work platforms behind machines in the No. 3 Forge and Machine Shops. One of the doors on a long worktable opened up. Inside the machinist had a six-foot bed made out of four inches of cotton waste with a makeshift pillow out of rags.

These guys worked on a type of incentive where they could accumulate extra time and then some would turn this time in on midnight shift. This way they made some incentive and got some sleep time.

I personally hated midnight shift. I would rather work real hard for eight hours on day shift, than come out on a midnight shift and do nothing.

WOMEN IN THE WORK PLACE

DURING THE FIRST WORLD WAR and the Second World War, the Bethlehem Steel Company had a problem recruiting new workers to manufacture the war materials that were being ordered by our government. The Steel was no different from many other plants across the country. Most of the young and eligible men were in the service of our country. Bethlehem Steel had to employ thousands of women to fill in the void left by the men.

The female workers did an exemplarily fine job. They did their job well. They boosted production and got the work out, but as soon as the war ended these women lost their jobs as the men came back to the work place and the jobs they had left behind. Also, many of the jobs that were related to the war effort, slowed down or shut down completely.

About the mid-seventies or so, equal work opportunities for women and ethnics were being pursued. Bethlehem Steel was urged to employ their fair share of female and ethnic workers.

When Bethlehem hired

Bethlehem Steel Corporation

Oxyacetylene welding, WWII era.

their first female workers they had next to no facilities for the women to wash in or, for that matter, toilet facilities. At first, the Steel installed some dead bolts on the doors of the toilet facilities. The female workers would just holler in to see if anyone was in there and then just walk right in. Most of the guys couldn't care less, but some male workers filed complaints when female workers walked right in while they were using the toilet or shower facilities.

In time some older washrooms were fixed up and used by the female workers only. The Steel also bought factory-made washroom trailers that were used by the female workers. Around most of the plant the women had to use the toilet facilities that their male counterparts used. Female facilities were few and far between.

At times there was flagrant disregard of some of the rules of behavior. One day while I was doing work at the Special Steel Depot in the Lehigh section of the plant, I couldn't believe my eyes on what I saw. As we were eating our lunch in the welfare room section, which was just off the toilet facilities, one of my buddies was using the urinal when a female janitor walked by him cleaning the floor in that area. I thought to myself, "Now I've seen it all."

Another time we riggers were doing work at the Sintering Plant. The riggers were using the sintering plant's welfare and washroom facilities. It was at quitting time and many of the workers were removing their clothes to take a shower. In one of the corners of the welfare room was an older Puerto Rican women who worked for the Sintering Plant as a laborer. One of her sideline duties was taking care of and making a large pot of coffee for the workers at the beginning of the shift.

This older women just sat there in the corner minding her own business. One of my buddies stopped by to talk to her. All she said was, "it's nothing that I didn't see before."

Most of the women did their jobs as well as their male counterparts. Yes, some were even better. Women were placed in many of the shops or departments but some just couldn't handle the jobs. Many quit while others took job transfers to jobs that were more compatible to women workers. Some female workers were tough as nails and could handle any type of work that the men could do. Others couldn't cut the mustard to save their souls.

I did have the opportunity to work with a few female workers. One particular female worker was just as good as many of the male workers. I had no problem having her on my crew. Yes, she had her moments, but don't we all?

Once all the cutbacks and buyouts are done, there will be very few female workers left in the plant itself.

(Opposite) Plant locomotive outside the Basic Oxygen Furnace, pushing one gondola and two sub cars.

CLOSE CALLS

WHILE I WAS WORKING as a chainman in the small run coming out of a small machine shop at Weldment in 1953, a chain broke and the piece of chain link whistled right on by. That was close.

In bay No. 3 of Weldment, I was chaining up a large storage type gas tank made by Buffalo Tank that had been brought in for repairs. As the crane was picking up the tank, the main crane's cable that goes through the block broke. The block crashed down, about three to five feet from where I was standing.

I was working on replacing gypsum/concrete roofs down in the mills, cutting out a large section of a roof with a small jackhammer with a spade, when a large section broke free and started falling toward the ground. I jumped to my right where there was a safety plank stretching between the purlins. If the plank hadn't been there I would have crashed about 35 feet to the ground.

Another time, while I was working on a rusted sheet-iron roof I broke through with both legs. Luckily there was a seam where the two sheets came together. This saved me from going clear down to the ground. Several other carpenters had similar experiences. One guy fell through a roof up in the press forge area but luckily he fell about 15 feet and landed on an overhead gas line. This stopped him from falling clear to the ground level.

In the late eighties, while I was working in the BOF vessel I smelled gas. Since this is an oxygen-type furnace there should be no gas. I hollered for the gang to get out of the vessel. When I complained to the BOF supervisors they claimed it

Joseph Elliott

(Above) Dismantling the No. 14 Press to repair the crack in the entablature. This was a 7,500-ton press, later upgraded to 10,000 tons and its designation changed to No. 1 Press.

(Left) A heating furnace in No. 2 Press Forge, where the 10,000-ton press is located.

was impossible for gas to be in the vessel. It seemed that the flame on a 2- to 3-inch coke line that pre-heats the ladles had gone out, and all the gas went from the ground up to the floor we were working on and was drawn down into the vessel. From that point on gas checkers had to check out the vessels whenever we worked in them. Through the years several workers died from different types of gas poisoning.

Unwise Work Procedures

While in the carpenters and the rigger gang, I helped to install a lot of machinery, which included different sizes of presses.

I found out through the engineers or the head supervision that no matter how big or how much power certain presses had that we installed in the past, the supervisors of that shop always pushed the machinery or presses beyond their limit. What would happen is that many small stress cracks would show up in the main structure of the press. Many times the hydraulic pumps would have their seals broken by excessive pressure that was way beyond what should have been used.

A Major Screw-up!

Up in the press forge, one supervisor sold the idea to other supervisors that they could save a bundle of money on heating fuel and man-hours by pressing ingots or other forgings colder than they were supposed to be done.

Instead of leaving them in the preheat furnaces until the required time, they brought them out earlier. In some cases, when the steel castings or forgings were cooling down and should have been returned to the preheating furnaces to be heated again, they kept pressing or moulding them to the desired shape.

At first this process worked. They got the finished forging out quicker and saved a bundle on heating-fuel costs.

Down the line, someone noticed cracks forming in the press's head or crown (the entablature). The company had their own engineers evaluate the damage. The conclusion was that it would take considerable work to repair the damages, and that the repairs had to be done immediately. Removing the head from the press was no easy matter.

Once removed, the piece was set up and preheated with large heating torches. All the cracks, from the smallest hair cracks to the large ones, had to be air-arced out. Then started the tedious task of filling in all the

Milling the bottom platen (base) of the press forge during repairs necessitated by cracking of the entablature. 1971.

cracks, pass by pass. Each pass had to be done properly and all slag removed. The welders had to work under very hot and strenous conditions. This took several weeks and a lot of man-hours. Even at that time, no one was sure if the new welds would work. Fortunately for the press forge, the welds held.

I don't know what happened to the supervisor who came up with this bad idea in the first place. It is possible that this goof-up was covered up so that the corporation's head people never found out why the cracks formed in the first place. I had seen in the past where supervisors screwed up royal, only to be promoted to better jobs.

THE ENDING OF A CAREER AND OF
THE HOT END OF THE BETHLEHEM PLANT

I TOO HAVE AGED, and just like the Grand Old Matriarch of the Bethlehem Steel Corporation, I also have seen better days. Two torn knees and two torn rotator cuffs in my shoulders have left me with some painful memories of the years past. Would I do it again? You bet!

In 1952 I graduated from Lansford High School and after a short vacation, started my illustrious career of forty years. Unlike many other steel company workers, I had the opportunity to work for about ten different departments. Being in the carpenters and the rigger departments I worked from one end of the plant to the other. I've seen it all. I also learned through my observations how many of the departments operated.

Yes, there were good times and bad times. I saw happy times and felt sad times when certain fellow workers or buddies died. I saw a few who couldn't wait until they went on pension, only to die before receiving their first check. I also saw quite a few live only a short time after pension. The average life span of most steel workers isn't too great. Stress, breathing toxic fumes, dirt and pollution didn't help.

For those 40 years that I gave to the company, I gave it my best. I do honestly feel that they got their money's worth out of me. Most of the other steel workers have this same feeling. There were many times that stress set in, but I bit the bullet and persevered.

Down through the years I saw where supervision took care of their own, because of friendship or ethnic reasons. I also saw throughout the years where some workers were taken care of and given promotions and more overtime than others because of the above. Supervision hasn't always been fair but this wasn't company policy, it was at the lower shop or department levels.

I do consider the Bethlehem Steel plant at Bethlehem as the Matriarch of the whole Bethlehem Steel Corporation. This grand old lady treated me fairly and I had a good life with her. We both had good times and bad times together. I never regretted our relationship for these past 40 years.

I just think that in its golden years this "Super Giant" is not getting a fair deal and it certainly is not having a very befitting ending. I said this before in this book and I am going to say it one more time. I think that some of the top managerial people fail to remember that it was this Bethlehem plant that made this corporation into what it is today.

In a short time from now this "Grand Old Lady" of the steelmaking industry will be nothing more than memories.

Never to be seen again in Bethlehem — a charging ladle dumping molten iron into the BOF. The last charge was on November 18, 1995.

TRIBUTE TO THE "GRAND OLD LADY" OF THE STEEL INDUSTRY

I do thank you, "Dear Lady," for giving me and all your employees the opportunity of serving you, to grow old with you, and in some cases, to die for you. We do know the pain and anguish that you are feeling from what the head corporate people are now doing to you. You can hold your head high and you can certainly be proud of all your past accomplishments throughout the years. You proved yourself well, time and time again.

Many families throughout the valley and elsewhere have depended on you and relied on you for raising families, for educating their sons and daughters, and last but not least, for the opportunity of living a good life. Some families had four or five generations of workers under your employment. When these employees talk about this, you can feel and sense the pride of this association.

I and all your faithful employees, past and present, tip our hats to you. You will always be considered the "Number One Steel Company" in our hearts and minds.